D0527355

AS

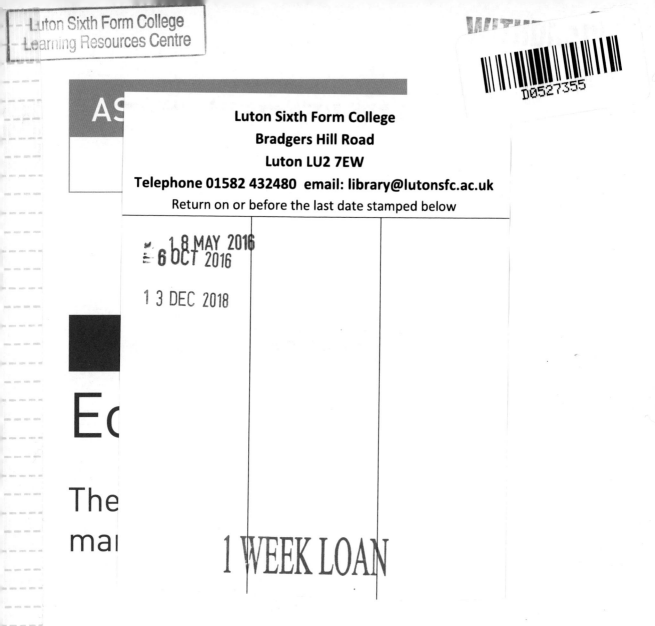

Ec

The

ma

Ray Powell and James Powell

WITHDRAWN 6 JAN 2016

Philip Allan, an imprint of Hodder Education, an Hachette UK company, Blenheim Court, George Street, Banbury, Oxfordshire OX16 5BH

**Orders**

Bookpoint Ltd, 130 Park Drive, Milton Park, Abingdon, Oxfordshire OX14 4SB

tel: 01235 827827

fax: 01235 400401

e-mail: education@bookpoint.co.uk

Lines are open 9.00 a.m.–5.00 p.m., Monday to Saturday, with a 24-hour message answering service. You can also order through the Hodder Education website: www.hoddereducation.co.uk

© Ray Powell and James Powell 2015

ISBN 978-1-4718-4330-3

First printed 2015

Impression number 5 4 3 2 1

Year 2019 2018 2017 2016 2015

This guide has been written specifically to support students preparing for the AQA AS and A-level Economics examinations. The content has been neither approved nor endorsed by AQA and remains the sole responsibility of the author.

Typeset by Integra Software Services Pvt. Ltd., Pondicherry, India

Cover photo: gui yong nian/Fotolia

Printed in Italy

Hachette UK's policy is to use papers that are natural, renewable and recyclable products and made from wood grown in sustainable forests. The logging and manufacturing processes are expected to conform to the environmental regulations of the country of origin.

# Contents

## Content Guidance

## Questions & Answers

### Multiple-choice questions

### Data-response questions

# ■ Getting the most from this book

## Exam tips

Advice on key points in the text to help you learn and recall content, avoid pitfalls, and polish your exam technique in order to boost your grade.

## Knowledge check

Rapid-fire questions throughout the Content Guidance section to check your understanding.

## Knowledge check answers

1 Turn to the back of the book for the Knowledge check answers.

## Summaries

■ Each core topic is rounded off by a bullet-list summary for quick-check reference of what you need to know.

**Exam-style questions**

**Commentary on the questions**

Tips on what you need to do to gain full marks, indicated by the icon

**Sample student answers**

Practise the questions, then look at the student answers that follow.

**Commentary on sample student answers**

Find out how many marks each answer would be awarded in the exam and then read the comments (preceded by the icon **e**) following each student answer.

---

Questions & Answers

**[24]** Lines 14–16 of Extract B state that from the start of 2009 until mid-2011, the price of pecan nuts rose from under $4.00 a pound to $7.50 a pound. Draw a supply and demand diagram to show the effect of a change in demand or supply conditions on the world price of pecan nuts over this period. [4 marks]

**e** All you need do when answering [04] questions is to draw a diagram in the space provided in the answer book.

**[25]** Making use of the information in Extract C, explain two possible reasons for changes in the world price of chocolate bars. [10 marks]

**e** Part [05] questions ask for 'explanation', but not for 'evaluation'. You will be wasting time if you try to evaluate the points you are making.

**[26]** Lines 23–28 of Extract C state that other chocolate manufacturers fear that Ferrero Rocher may exploit its monopoly power and deny competitors access to Turkish hazelnuts. Evaluate the view that if Ferrero Rocher exercises its monopoly power, market failure will inevitably occur. [25 marks]

**e** Look out for words such as 'inevitably' in the question. If you ignore such a word, your evaluation is going to be limited and the mark for your answer will probably not rise above Level 3 [11–15 marks out of 25].

### Student A

**[21]** The movement of the whole of a supply curve to a new position, either to the left or right of the original supply curve.

**e** 3/3 marks awarded. An accurate definition of a shift of a supply curve.

**[22]** The answer is 655%.

**e** 4/4 marks awarded. An accurate calculation with the unit of measurement provided.

**[23]** The price of pecan nuts ranged between a maximum of just over $7.50 a pound in early summer and early autumn 2011 from a low of about $3.80 a pound at the beginning of the data series in January 2009. A second significant feature was continuing volatility in the price of pecan nuts throughout the data period, for example with the price falling from about $6.25 a pound in October 2010 to $6.00 a pound at the end of December 2010, before rising to $7.00 a pound in the next month in January 2011.

**e** 4/4 marks awarded. Two significant features of the data are identified, with full statistical back-up. Although the answer is written clearly, it would be helpful to the examiner to start a second paragraph for the second feature identified.

# ■ About this book

The aim of this guide is to prepare students for the AQA AS Paper 1, 'The operation of markets and market failure', examination and for parts of the AQA A-level Paper 1, 'Markets and market failure', examination. The parts of the AQA A-level Paper 1 not covered in this guide are covered in Student Guide 3. Remember also that all the topics explained in this book could be examined in the A-level Paper 3, which is a synoptic paper testing the whole of the A-level specification.

## Content Guidance

Start off by reading the Content Guidance section of the book, which covers five separate topics. You can read all the topics, one by one, before proceeding to the Questions & Answers section of the guide. Alternatively, you may decide to read a particular topic and then to read the corresponding part of the Questions & Answers section. The topics follow the order of the AS Part 1 specification, starting from 'Economic methodology and the economic problem' and finishing with 'The market mechanism, market failure and government intervention in markets'.

## Questions & Answers

You should read the Questions & Answers section of the book either after reading all five specification topics in the Content Guidance section or bit by bit, having revised a selected topic on a particular part of the specification.

## Multiple-choice questions (MCQs)

There are ten multiple-choice questions (MCQs) and six data-response questions (DRQs) in the Questions & Answers section of the guide. There are two MCQs on each of the five topics covered by the guide. The questions are typical of those commonly set on each of the five topics covered in the Content Guidance section of the guide. Each of these questions is similar in layout, structure and style to an MCQ in AS Paper 1 and A-level Paper 3 (A-level Paper 1 does not include MCQs). A commentary has been included after each question to explain the correct answer and any other important features of the question.

## Data-response questions (DRQs)

The ten MCQs are followed by six data-response questions. You can use the DRQs either as timed test questions in the lead-up to the examination or to reinforce your understanding of the specification subject matter, topic by topic, as you proceed through the Content Guidance. In this guide, the data-response questions are numbered 1 to 6, but in the exams the two questions will be numbered either Context 1 or Context 2. Three of the questions in this book are in the style of AS context questions; the other three are in the style of A-level context questions. (Both AS Paper 1 and A-level Paper 1 require you to answer just one of the two context DRQs in the paper.)

This section, covering the data-response questions, also includes:

■ a student answer for each DRQ
■ comments on each student's answer explaining, where relevant, how the answer could be improved. These comments are denoted by the icon **ⓔ**.

This guide should be used as a supplement to other resources, such as class notes, textbooks, *Economic Review* magazine and *AS/A-level Economics Exam Revision Notes*. (The last two of these are published by Philip Allan for Hodder Education.) As this guide contains summaries rather than in-depth coverage of all the topics in the specification, you should not use the guide as your sole learning resource during the main part of the course. However, you may well decide to use the guide as the key resource in your revision programme. You are strongly advised to make full use of the Questions & Answers section, especially in the revision period when you should be concentrating on improving your examination skills.

# Content Guidance

# ■ Summary of the specification

The AQA AS specification for 'The operation of markets and market failure' contains the following five sections:

- 3.1.1 Economic methodology and the economic problem
- 3.1.2 Price determination in a competitive market
- 3.1.3 Production, costs and revenue
- 3.1.4 Competitive and concentrated markets
- 3.1.5 The market mechanism, market failure and government intervention in markets

These also figure in the A-level specification for 'Markets and market failure', though the A-level specification also includes topics covered in Student Guide 3 and not in this guide.

## 3.1.1 Economic methodology and the economic problem

How can you decide whether a market performs well or badly? You must assess the extent to which the market contributes to the solution of the economic problem, which is part of the title of both the first section of the specification and the first topic in this guide. A market performs well when the price mechanism, operating within the market, solves to a satisfactory degree the economic problem of scarcity. By contrast, if the price mechanism (or market mechanism) functions unsatisfactorily (or, in extreme cases, breaks down completely and fails to function at all), market failure occurs. Some resources which appear to be 'free' and available in unlimited supply are in fact scarce. The environment is an example of such a scarce resource, and its scarcity is affected by many of the economic decisions made by human beings.

The central purpose of economic activity is to improve economic welfare (which can be thought of as happiness enjoyed by the whole population). For the most part, improving economic welfare requires production of goods and services so that people's needs and wants can be satisfied. The production of goods and services in turn means that certain questions have to be addressed, such as what to produce, how to produce and for whom to produce.

The key concepts you must know that relate to the economic problem of scarcity are the nature of economic resources or factors of production (land, labour, capital and enterprise), the importance of choice, opportunity cost, and the assumption that all economic agents (households, firms and the government) have objectives that they wish to maximise. You must also understand the difference between free goods and economic goods. Production possibility curves can be used to illustrate the economic problem and another key concept in section 3.1.1: opportunity cost.

As its title indicates, the specification section starts off by introducing you to the methodology of economics. This includes recognition of value judgements and understanding the difference between positive statements (statements of fact or statements that can be shown to be either true or false) and normative statements (statements of opinion).

# 3.1.2 Price determination in a competitive market

This is a core area of the specification, at the centre of which is the supply and demand economic model. To meet the requirements of this section of the specification, you must learn, understand and be able to apply important terms and concepts such as demand, supply, equilibrium, disequilibrium, elasticity, and the signalling, incentive and rationing functions of prices. Make sure you can apply elasticity formulae to calculate price elasticity of demand, income elasticity of demand, cross elasticity of demand and price elasticity of supply. You must understand the difference between a shift of a demand or supply curve and an adjustment along a supply or demand curve in response to a price change. Practise drawing supply and demand diagrams to illustrate shifts of supply and demand caused by changes in factors, other than price, that determine supply and demand. You must learn to apply your knowledge of the basic model of demand and supply to markets, including commodity markets such as oil and copper markets, agriculture, healthcare, housing, sport and leisure.

Probably the most important skill you must learn when studying this section of the specification is applying demand and supply analysis to particular markets. This is a key skill tested in the Paper 1 examinations at both AS and A-level.

# 3.1.3 Production, costs and revenue

As already mentioned, throughout your studies you must always remember that improved economic welfare is the ultimate purpose of economic activity, but that production of more goods and services is usually necessary for welfare to improve. In order to maximise welfare, production must take place efficiently rather than inefficiently. You must understand and learn to apply the concept of productive efficiency, which involves maximising output of goods and services from available inputs (the economic resources or factors of production mentioned in section 3.1.1). While productive efficiency is an A-level rather than an AS concept, it is nevertheless useful to understand at AS.

Two factors that increase productive efficiency are specialisation and economies of scale. Specialisation, which occurs when different industries produce different goods and services, leads to the growth of trade and exchange. Economies of scale, which result from the growth in size of firms and industries, lead to falling average costs of production and to an increase in productive efficiency. By contrast, diseconomies of scale, which involve rising average costs as the scale of a firm increases, result in productive inefficiency. Diseconomies of scale discourage any further growth of a firm. For a firm, productive efficiency occurs when economies of scale have been achieved to the full, but before any possible diseconomies of scale set in.

The economy as a whole is productively efficient when production takes place on the economy's production possibility frontier or boundary. In this situation, it is impossible to increase production of one good without reducing production of one or more other goods.

# 3.1.4 Competitive and concentrated markets

This section of the AS and A-level specifications introduces you to the two extreme market structures of perfect competition and monopoly, both of which are examined in more depth in Student Guide 3. Monopoly is the most concentrated form of market structure, since there is only one firm in the market. There are, however, other types of concentrated market which are examples of imperfectly competitive markets. The degree of market concentration can be measured using a concentration ratio. In the AS and A-level Paper 1 exams you may be asked to calculate a concentration ratio as part of a test of your quantitative skills and ability to perform calculations. All the market structures that lie between the two extremes of perfect competition and pure monopoly are examples of imperfect competition, a topic which is explained in more depth in Student Guide 3.

The topic of competitive and concentrated markets covers the distinctions between monopoly and monopoly power, and between different forms of competition such as price competition and non-price competition. The latter includes quality competition.

# 3.1.5 The market mechanism, market failure and government intervention in markets

The first topic in this section of the AS and A-level specifications centres on the functions prices perform in resource allocation within markets. This then leads into the key topic of market failure. Markets may fail either because they perform inequitably (unfairly or unjustly) or because they perform inefficiently. Different people have different opinions about what is fair, so the first type of market failure depends on normative views or value judgements, explained earlier in section 3.1.1. Many economists argue that inequalities in the distributions of income and wealth provide a significant example of market failure resulting from markets performing inequitably. Whenever markets are productively inefficient, or when they misallocate resources between competing uses, the second type of market failure occurs. Monopoly, explained in section 3.1.4, is an important example. If the incentive function of prices breaks down completely, markets may be unable to produce any quantity of a good. Public goods provide an example, and there are also 'missing markets' in externalities. In other cases, markets may succeed in providing a good but end up providing the 'wrong' quantity. This happens if the market price is too high, which discourages consumption, or too low, which has the opposite effect of encouraging too much consumption. The main examples are merit and demerit goods.

Immobility of factors of production is also likely to lead to a misallocation of resources and therefore cause market failure.

When analysing the role of the state in the economy, economists usually assume that governments wish to maximise social welfare (i.e. the public interest or the economic welfare of the whole community).

When intervening in the market, governments have various policy instruments at their disposal. The most extreme method of intervention involves abolishing the market, such as when the government provides public and merit goods directly and finances their provision through the tax system. At the other extreme, governments often allow markets to function largely free of intervention, but modified to some extent by the effect of taxes or minor regulation. Taxation and regulation are the main forms of government intervention in markets. Other methods of intervention cited in the specification include subsidies, price controls and, in the case of negative externalities, permits to pollute.

You might also be asked to explain, analyse and assess the effectiveness of intervention in the form of price ceilings or price floors. Much government intervention attempts to correct the various market failures already mentioned. However, an attempt to correct market failure can lead to government failure. First, government intervention to correct a market failure or to achieve the government's objectives may simply be unsuccessful. Second, and often more seriously, completely new economic problems may emerge as a direct result of government intervention trying to correct other problems.

# ■3.1.1 Economic methodology and the economic problem

These notes relate to AQA specification section 3.1.1 and prepare you to answer examination questions on:
- economic methodology
- the nature and purpose of economic activity
- economic resources
- scarcity, choice and the allocation of resources
- production possibility diagrams

## Essential information

### Economic methodology

When answering the question 'What is economics?' a good starting point is the fact that economics is a social science. Social science is the branch of science that studies society and the relationships of individuals within a society.

Like other social scientists in subjects such as psychology, economists start off by observing some aspect of human behaviour and then try to develop a theory from what they have observed. In the case of production theory, the starting point is observations of how firms react to changes in the prices of the goods and services they sell. Production theory then develops from establishing a tentative description, known as a hypothesis, of what has been observed. Predictions about human behaviour are deduced from the hypothesis, such as that the owner of a firm will always respond to the price of a good rising by supplying more of the good in question. This prediction is then tested against collected evidence about how firms behave in the market place. At this stage, the hypothesis becomes a *theory*. (A hypothesis is a proposed explanation for something, whereas a theory is when a hypothesis is tested and survives the test.) Nevertheless, a theory may not be true in all circumstances. All it says is that the hypothesis has survived the test or tests to which it has been exposed; it might not survive stronger tests, which may not yet have been devised. Scientific method is based on the possibility of falsification or refutation of a hypothesis.

A lot of economics is concerned with what people ought to do. Ought people to pay for goods and not steal? Such a question falls within the remit of normative economics. Normative economics is about value judgements and opinions, but because people have different opinions about what is right and wrong, normative statements cannot be scientifically tested: they are just opinions.

By contrast, a positive statement can be scientifically tested to see whether it is incorrect. If a positive statement does not pass the test, it is falsified. However, a positive statement does not have to be true. For example, 'the earth is flat' is a positive statement. A few people may believe it, though obviously with the growth of scientific evidence the statement has been falsified. The key point is that while positive statements can in principle be tested and possibly falsified, normative statements cannot. Words such as 'ought', 'should', 'better', 'worse', 'good' and 'bad' (used as adjectives) often provide clues that a statement is normative.

## The nature and purpose of economic activity

The ultimate purpose or objective of economic activity is to increase people's happiness or **economic welfare**. Increased production enables economic welfare to improve, but only if the production of more goods and services leads to higher levels of consumption. Production and consumption often result in resource depletion (using up scarce resources) and resource degradation (e.g. pollution and destruction of the natural environment).

**Economic welfare** The economic well-being of an individual, a group within society or an economy.

As a general rule, consumption improves economic welfare and people's standard of living (although in certain circumstances consumption can reduce rather than increase welfare). Economists often use the word 'utility' for the welfare that people enjoy when they consume goods and services. Goods such as food bought for consumption are known as consumer goods; by contrast, a good such as a machine bought by a firm in order to produce other goods is called a capital good. Goods that people produce for their own consumption, and activities such as contemplating the natural environment, contribute to people's utility or welfare, adding to the utility obtained from consuming goods bought in the market.

When discussing economic welfare, we need to distinguish between a **need** and a **want**. A need refers to something people have to have, something they cannot do without. Food is an example. If people starve, they will eventually die. By contrast, a want refers to something people would like to have but which is not essential for survival. It is not absolutely necessary, but it is a good thing to have.

**Needs and wants** A need is something that is necessary for human survival, such as food. A want is something that is desirable, such as ice cream, but is not necessary for human survival.

There are also important elements of human happiness and welfare that have nothing to do with the consumption of material goods. These include quality of life factors, such as the pleasure gained from family and friends or from contemplating a beautiful view.

## Economic resources

For most people, most of the time, increased consumption of material goods is an important part of improving economic welfare. Most, if not all, of the goods we consume must first be produced. This requires the use of economic resources. These goods are scarce in relation to demand, which gives rise to the need for economising in their use.

The inputs into the production process are often called the factors of production. Four factors of production are usually identified. These are land, labour, capital and enterprise, the last often being called the entrepreneurial input.

Entrepreneurs are different from the other factors of production. They are the people who address issues such as what to produce, how to produce it and for whom to produce it. An entrepreneur decides how much of the other factors of production, including labour, to employ. When making these decisions, the entrepreneur takes into account the financial risks involved. Profit, which is the entrepreneur's financial reward, results from successful decision making. Entrepreneurial profit is the profit left over after the cost of employing the other factors of production is deducted from the sales revenue gained from the sale of the goods and services the entrepreneur decides to produce.

## Scarcity, choice and the allocation of resources

Economics is literally the study of economising – the study of how human beings make choices about what to produce, how to produce and for whom to produce, in a world in which most of the resources are limited. Because resources are limited in relation to people's infinite wants, scarcity is the fundamental **economic problem**.

The fundamental economic problem exists because both goods and the resources needed to produce goods are scarce. Scarcity also means that people (even the very rich) have limited incomes and face a budget constraint. If goods are scarce and incomes are limited, choices have to be made. And even when goods are free, time is scarce, so choices still have to be made. A need for choice also arises whenever an economic agent (for example, an individual, a household or a firm) has to choose between two or more alternatives that are mutually exclusive, in the sense that it is impossible or impractical to achieve both at the same time.

## Production possibility diagrams

The key feature of a production possibility diagram is a production possibility frontier (*PPF*) or production possibility curve. A *PPF* curve illustrates the different combinations of two goods, or two sets of goods, that can be produced with a fixed quantity of resource, providing we assume that all available resources are being utilised to the full. The *PPF* curve in Figure 1 illustrates the different combinations of capital goods and consumer goods that the whole economy can produce when all the economy's resources are employed, with no spare capacity. To put it another way, the *PPF* curve shows what the economy can produce, assuming that all the labour, capital and land at the country's disposal are employed to the full, and assuming a given state of technical progress.

Suppose that initially the economy is at point $A$ on the frontier, producing $K_1$ capital goods and $C_1$ consumer goods. In the absence of economic growth (which moves the frontier outward), consumer good production can only increase to $C_2$ if the production of capital goods falls from to $K_1$ to $K_2$.

**Knowledge check 1**

What is meant by scarcity and economising?

The fall in the production of capital goods when the production of consumer goods increases is called an **opportunity cost**.

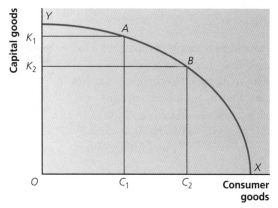

**Figure 1** An economy's production possibility frontier

Economists generally assume that people behave rationally. Rational behaviour means people try to make decisions in their self-interest or to maximise their private benefit. When a choice has to be made, people always choose what they think at the time is the best alternative, which means that the second best or next best alternative is rejected. Providing people are rational, the opportunity cost of any decision or choice is the next best alternative sacrificed or forgone. For example, if you choose to spend half an hour reading an economics textbook, the opportunity cost is the lost opportunity to spend that time watching a TV programme.

Production possibility frontier diagrams are often used to illustrate the concepts of **productive efficiency** and inefficiency. Productive efficiency occurs when output is maximised from available inputs. A *PPF* curve shows maximisation of output from available inputs at every point on the curve, though the combination of the two goods (in Figure 1 capital goods and consumer goods) varies at different points on the curve. This means that all points on the economy's production possibility frontier, including points *A* and *B*, are productively efficient. By contrast, all points inside the *PPF* curve are productively inefficient. Productive inefficiency occurs when output is not maximised from available inputs. When productively inefficient, the economy is not employing all its available resources.

# Examination skills

The skills most likely to be tested by multiple-choice and data-response questions on economic methodology and the economic problem, both at AS and the full A-level, are as follows:

- Interpreting and possibly drawing a production possibility diagram such as Figure 1.
- Understanding and explaining that the purpose of economic activity is to increase welfare.
- Understanding and explaining how the scenario of the question illustrates the problem of scarcity.
- Explaining and applying the concept of opportunity cost.
- Analysing an economic problem in terms of trade-offs between conflicting objectives.

**Opportunity cost** The opportunity cost of any decision is the next best alternative sacrificed or given up.

**Exam tip**

You must learn to draw and interpret production possibility diagrams, which are as important in macroeconomics as in microeconomics.

**Productive efficiency** Maximising output from available inputs.

■ Distinguishing between a statement of fact (a positive statement) and a value judgement (a normative statement).

# Examination questions

Knowledge and understanding of scarcity may be tested by multiple-choice questions in the contexts of production possibility frontiers and free goods. Because it is the central topic in economics, virtually every examination question in economics touches upon the economic problem and its related concepts. For the most part, specific knowledge of the economic problem will be tested by multiple-choice questions rather than by data-response questions. You should expect up to two multiple-choice questions on the terms and concepts listed in this chapter: MCQ 1 and MCQ 2 in the Questions & Answers section of this guide are typical examples.

## Common examination errors

Common mistakes on economic methodology and the economic problem include the following:

■ failure to appreciate that almost all problems and issues in economics involve the problem of scarcity and its related concepts
■ failure to relate scarcity to the need for rationing and to the role of rationing mechanisms such as the price mechanism and queues and waiting lists
■ inaccurate drawing of production possibility diagrams
■ not understanding the importance of opportunity cost in economic decision making
■ confusing positive and normative statements

**Knowledge check 2**

Give an example of an opportunity cost, other than the capital goods given up when the production of consumer goods increases.

---

## Summary

■ Economics is the study of economising.
■ Economics answers questions on what to produce, how to produce and for whom to produce, in a world in which most of the resources are limited relative to wants and needs.
■ Scarcity is the fundamental economic problem.
■ The production of economic goods uses up scarce resources and people have to economise in their use.

■ Scarcity of economic resources means opportunity costs exist and choices have to be made.
■ A production possibility frontier shows the different combinations of goods that can be produced from available resources.
■ A normative statement involves a value judgement whereas a positive statement can be tested to see whether it is true or false.

# 3.1.2 Price determination in a competitive market

These notes relate to AQA AS specification section 3.1.2 and A-level specification section 4.1.2 and prepare you to answer examination questions on the following:

- the determinants of the demand for goods and services
- price, income and cross elasticities of demand
- the determinants of the supply of goods and services
- price elasticity of supply
- the determination of equilibrium market prices
- the interrelationship between markets

## Essential information

### The determinants of the demand for goods and services

Normally when economists refer to demand, they mean **market demand**. This is the quantity of a good or service that all the consumers in the market wish to, and are able to, buy at different prices. Market demand is shown by a downward-sloping demand curve such as the one shown in Figure 2. However, the market demand curve is simply the sum of individual demand curves of each of the consumers in the market.

The law of demand states that as a good's price falls, more is demanded. There is thus an inverse relationship between price and quantity demanded. The market demand curve drawn in Figure 2 illustrates the law of demand. If the price starts off high, for example at $P_1$, household demand is $Q_1$. But if the price falls to $P_2$, demand increases to $Q_2$.

**Market demand** The quantity of a good or service that all the consumers in a market are willing and able to buy.

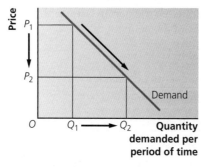

**Figure 2** A market demand curve

It is easy to confuse the difference between a movement along (or adjustment along) a demand curve and a shift of a demand curve. When we draw a market demand curve to show how much of the good or service households plan to demand at various possible prices, we assume that all the other variables that may also influence demand are held unchanged or constant.

For example, an increase in income shifts demand curves rightward – but only for normal goods. A **normal good** is defined as a good for which demand increases when

**Normal good** Demand for the good increases as income increases.

income increases. By contrast, an **inferior good** is a good (such as poor-quality food) for which demand falls as income increases. If the good is inferior, an increase in income shifts the demand curve leftward. Figure 3 shows a rightward shift of demand from $D_1$ to $D_2$, caused perhaps by a fall in the price of a good in joint demand (a complementary good) or by a successful advertising campaign for the product. The figure shows that at price $P_1$, demand has increased from $Q_1$ to $Q_2$.

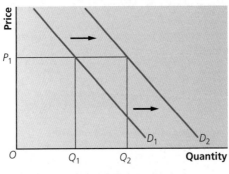

**Figure 3** The effect of a rightward shift of demand in a market

**Inferior good** Demand for the good falls as income increases.

**Knowledge check 3**

Explain the difference between a shift of demand and an adjustment of demand.

**Exam tip**

Exam questions often test whether you can distinguish between a shift of demand or supply and an adjustment of demand or supply along a demand or supply curve.

## Price, income and cross elasticities of demand

Whenever a change in one variable (such as a good's price) causes a change to occur in a second variable (such as the quantity of the good that consumers are prepared to demand), an elasticity can be calculated. Elasticity measures the proportionate response or change in a second variable following an initial change in a first variable. For example, if a 5% increase in price were to cause consumers to reduce their demand more than proportionately (say, by 10%), demand would be price elastic. If the response were less than proportionate (for example, a fall in demand of only 3%), demand would be price inelastic. And if the change in price were to induce an exactly proportionate change in demand, demand would be neither elastic nor inelastic with respect to the price change – this is called unit elasticity of demand.

The formulae for the three demand elasticities you need to know are:

$$\text{Price elasticity of demand} = \frac{\text{Proportionate change in quantity demanded}}{\text{Proportionate change in price}}$$

$$\text{Income elasticity of demand} = \frac{\text{Proportionate change in quantity demanded}}{\text{Proportionate change in income}}$$

$$\text{Cross elasticity of demand for good A with respect to the price of B} = \frac{\text{Proportionate change in quantity of A demanded}}{\text{Proportionate change in price of B}}$$

### Price elasticity of demand

Price elasticity of demand measures consumers' responsiveness to a change in a good's price. The factors that influence price elasticity of demand are:

- Substitutability: this is the most important determinant of price elasticity of demand. When a substitute exists for a product, consumers can respond to a price rise by switching expenditure away from the good, buying instead the substitute whose price has not risen. Demand for necessities tends to be inelastic as they have few substitutes. A substitute good is a good that can be used instead of another good, e.g. apples as a substitute for pears.

- Percentage of income: goods or services upon which households spend a large proportion of their income tend to be in more elastic demand than small items upon which only a fraction of income is spent.
- The 'width' of the market definition: the demand for Shell petrol is much more price elastic than the market demand for petrol produced by all the oil companies.
- Time: although there are exceptions, demand for many goods and services is more elastic in the long run than in the short run because it takes time to respond to a price change.

### Income elasticity of demand

Income elasticity of demand – which measures how demand responds to a change in income – is always negative for an inferior good and positive for a normal good. The quantity demanded of an inferior good falls as income rises, whereas demand for a normal good rises with income. Normal goods are sometimes further subdivided into superior goods or luxuries, for which the income elasticity of demand is greater than unity, and basic goods, with an income elasticity of less than 1.

### Cross elasticity of demand

Cross elasticity of demand measures the responsiveness of demand for one commodity to changes in the price of another good. The cross elasticity of demand between two goods or services indicates the nature of the demand relationship between the goods. There are three possibilities: joint demand (negative cross elasticity), competing demand or substitutes (positive cross elasticity) and an absence of any discernible demand relationship (zero cross elasticity).

## The determinants of the supply of goods and services

**Market supply** is the quantity of a good or service that all the firms or producers in the market plan to sell at different prices.

The market supply curve in Figure 4 illustrates the law of supply, which states that as a good's price rises, more is supplied. If the price starts off low, for example at $P_1$, firms are willing to supply $Q_1$. But if the price rises to $P_2$, planned supply increases to $Q_2$.

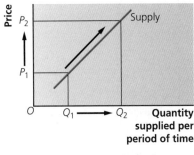

**Figure 4** A market supply curve

A market supply curve shows the quantities of the good that all the firms in the market plan to supply at different possible prices, assuming the conditions of supply remain unchanged. If a condition of supply changes, the supply curve shifts to a new position. A rightward shift of supply is also known as an increase in supply, whereas a leftward shift is known as a decrease in supply.

The main conditions of supply are costs of production (which include costs of wages, raw materials, energy and borrowing costs), technical progress, taxes imposed on firms, such as VAT, excise duties and the business rate, and government subsidies granted to firms.

## Price elasticity of supply

In contrast to demand elasticities explained earlier, there is only one supply elasticity you need to know. This is **price elasticity of supply**, which measures how the supply of a good responds to an initial change in a good's price.

The formula for price elasticity of supply is:

$$\text{Price elasticity of supply} = \frac{\text{Proportionate change in quantity supplied}}{\text{Proportionate change in price}}$$

The main factors determining price elasticity of supply are the length of the production period, the availability of spare capacity, the ease of accumulating stocks, both of raw materials needed for production to take place and of finished goods waiting to be sold, the ease of switching between alternative methods of production, the number of firms in the market and the ease of entering the market, and finally the time period in question.

> **Price elasticity of supply** The proportionate change in supply of a good following an initial proportionate change in the good's price.

## The determination of equilibrium market prices

Before explaining the determination of equilibrium market prices, we must define a market. A market, which is simply a voluntary meeting of buyers and sellers, is highly competitive when there is a very large number of buyers and sellers all passively accepting the ruling market price set, not by individual decisions but by the interaction of all those taking part in the market. Figure 5 illustrates the key features of a competitive market.

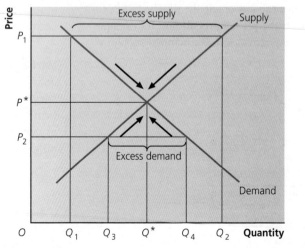

**Figure 5** The price mechanism operating within a market

The demand curve shows the quantities of a good that households or consumers plan to purchase at different prices, and the supply curve shows how much firms or producers plan to supply at different prices. At all prices (except the equilibrium price) it is impossible for both households and firms simultaneously to fulfil their market plans. For example, at price $P_1$ firms would like to supply $Q_2$, but households are only willing to purchase $Q_1$. Planned supply is greater than planned demand, resulting in an excess supply. By contrast, at price $P_2$ households wish to buy $Q_4$ but firms restrict supply to $Q_3$ and excess demand results. At any price other than $P^*$, which is the **equilibrium price**, there will be either excess supply or excess demand, with either the firms or the households unable to fulfil their market plans. The market is in disequilibrium when there is excess supply or excess demand.

We now assume that firms respond to excess supply by reducing the price they are prepared to accept, while conversely households bid up the price to eliminate excess demand. The price falls or rises until equilibrium is achieved. The equilibrium price is the only price that satisfies both households and firms, which consequently have no reason to change their market plans. At $P^*$ planned demand = planned supply.

Three conditions are necessary for a market to operate successfully:

- The individual buyers and sellers decide what, how, how much, where and when to trade or exchange.
- They do so with reference to their self-interest and to the alternatives or opportunities open to them. The exchange must be voluntary; if one party forces a transaction upon the other, it is not a market transaction.
- Prices convey information to buyers and sellers about self-interest and opportunities. For a market to allocate resources among different types of activity and to coordinate economic activity throughout the economy, prices must respond to the forces of supply and demand.

Nearly 250 years ago, the great classical economist Adam Smith, who is often called the 'father of economics', described how the invisible or hidden hand of the market, operating in competitive markets and through the pursuit of self-interest, achieves an allocation of resources that is also in society's interest. This remains the central view of all **free-market economists**, i.e. those who believe in the virtues of a competitive market economy subject to minimum government intervention.

## The interrelationship between markets

So far we have looked at how the price mechanism operates in a competitive market. We have seen how shifts of either the demand curve for the good or the good's supply curve disturb market equilibrium and trigger an adjustment process to establish a new equilibrium.

Very often shifts of curves are caused by events taking place in other markets in the economy. They can be caused by a change of price of a good in joint supply or, on the demand side, by a change in the price of a good in joint demand, a substitute good, a good in composite demand, or a good in derived demand.

Joint supply occurs when production of one good also leads to the supply of a byproduct. For example, a rise in the price of one of the two goods in joint supply leads to a shift of the supply curve of the other good. Competing supply, meanwhile,

**Equilibrium price** The price that clears the market, at which there is no excess demand or excess supply.

**Knowledge check 7**

What is meant by equilibrium in economics?

**Exam tip**

Equilibrium and its opposite, disequilibrium, are two of the most important economic concepts you need to understand.

**Free-market economists** Those who believe that resource allocation should be left solely or mostly to the market mechanism (or price mechanism) and to private enterprise or free enterprise.

occurs when, because raw materials are used to produce one good, they cannot be used to produce another good.

When the supply curve of a good shifts, for example because of a joint supply or competing supply relationship with a good produced and sold in another market, the extent to which price and quantity respectively change in the market depends on price elasticity of demand for the good. The possibilities are shown in Figure 6.

**Exam tip**

When you explain events occurring in a market, it is often relevant to discuss the price elasticity of the demand curve and/or the supply curve.

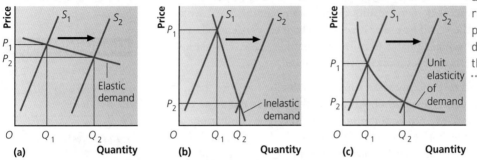

**Figure 6** The extent to which price and quantity change following a shift of supply depends upon price elasticity of demand

When demand is elastic (Figure 6a), the quantity bought and sold adjusts much more than price. The reverse is true when demand is inelastic (Figure 6b). Finally, when demand is unit elastic (depicted in the rectangular hyperbola in Figure 6c), price and quantity change by equal percentages.

An increase in the price of a good in joint demand (or a **complementary good**) has the opposite effect to an increase in the price of a **substitute good** (or a good in competing demand). Figure 7 shows a rightward shift of demand from $D_1$ to $D_2$, caused perhaps by a fall in the price of a good in joint demand (a complementary good) or by a rise in the price of a substitute good. Before the shift of demand, $P_1$ was the equilibrium price. Following the shift of demand, this is no longer the case. Planned demand is greater than planned supply and there is excess demand of $Q_2$ minus $Q_1$ in the market. To relieve the excess demand, the price rises to a new equilibrium at $P_2$.

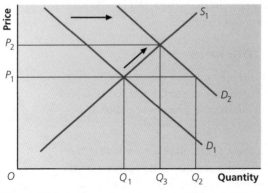

**Figure 7** The effect of a rightward shift of demand in a market

It is easy to confuse competing demand, which occurs when two goods are substitutes, with **composite demand** and **derived demand**. Composite demand is demand for a

**Complementary goods** Goods that are in joint demand (they go together), such as cars and petrol.

**Substitute goods** Goods that are in competing demand, such as Sony and Nintendo games consoles.

**Composite demand** Demand for a good that has more than one use.

**Derived demand** Demand for a good that is an input into the production of another good.

good that has more than one use. This means that an increase in demand for one use of the good reduces the supply of the good for an alternative use. By contrast, derived demand for a good occurs when a good is necessary for the production of other goods. The demand for capital goods such as machinery and raw materials is derived from the demand for consumer goods or finished goods. If the demand for cars falls, so does the demand for car components such as tyres.

**Knowledge check 8**

Give another example of a good that is in composite demand.

# Examination skills

The skills most likely to be tested by multiple-choice and data-response questions on price determination in a competitive market are as follows:

- Interpreting a graph or table to describe the changes taking place over a period of time in the price of a good.
- Interpreting a graph or table to compare changes in the prices of two goods.
- Drawing a supply and demand diagram to illustrate the market in equilibrium.
- Identifying a change in either the conditions of demand or the conditions of supply, and the resulting shift of either the demand curve or the supply curve.
- Explaining how the market mechanism operates to eliminate excess demand or excess supply, and the adjustment of the market to a new equilibrium.
- Distinguishing between a shift of a demand or supply curve and an adjustment in response to a price change along a demand or supply curve.
- Analysing goods in joint demand (complementary goods, such as cars and petrol), competing demand (substitute goods, such as tea and coffee) and joint supply (such as beef and leather).

# Examination questions

In AS paper 1, you should expect up to six of the 20 multiple-choice questions to be set on price determination in a competitive market, including at least two on elasticity. In A-level Paper 3, you should expect at least one of the 30 multiple-choice questions (covering both microeconomics and macroeconomics) to be on price determination in a competitive market. MCQ 3 in the Questions & Answers section of this guide is a typical example of a question on the effect of a shift of a demand curve. Question 4 is typical of a question testing understanding of price and cross elasticities of demand. Supply and demand is also likely to figure prominently in at least one of the two optional data-response questions in the AS Paper 1 exam. In the A-level Paper 1 exam, a part or parts of one of the two data questions may be on price determination in a competitive market, but the whole of a question is unlikely to be devoted to the topic. DRQ 1, on markets for nuts, is typical of an AS question on the functioning of markets. The markets that figure in AS DRQs are quite likely to be markets for primary products such as agricultural commodities, oil and metals.

# Common examination errors

Commonly made mistakes on price determination in a competitive market include the following:

- Confusing a shift of a demand curve with an adjustment along a demand curve (likewise, confusing a shift of a supply curve with an adjustment along a supply curve).

- Confusing the factors that cause a demand curve to shift with those that cause a supply curve to shift.
- Drawing supply and demand graphs with the curves and axes wrongly labelled.
- Confusing excess demand and excess supply.
- Confusing elasticity with slope. By definition, straight-line demand and supply curves have constant slopes, but elasticity varies from point to point along many (though not all) demand and supply curves.
- Missing out the word 'proportionate' or 'percentage' in elasticity formulae (as in 'proportionate change in quantity demanded').
- Confusing normal goods and inferior goods when a change in income causes a demand curve to shift.
- Confusing composite demand and derived demand with other demand concepts such as joint demand.

## Summary

- A market is a meeting of buyers and sellers for the purpose of exchanging goods or services.
- Two of the main features of a market are a demand curve and a supply curve.
- Market equilibrium occurs when demand equals supply.
- Disequilibrium in a market means there is either excess demand or excess supply in the market.
- In a competitive market, the market mechanism (or price mechanism) causes the price to rise or fall to get rid of excess demand or excess supply.
- Market equilibrium may be disturbed by a shift in either the demand curve or the supply curve.
- A change in a condition of demand, such as consumers' incomes, causes the demand curve to shift to a new position.
- Likewise, a change in a condition of supply, such as costs of production, causes the supply curve to shift to a new position.
- Joint demand is when two goods are demanded together; competing demand is when two goods are substitutes for each other.
- Composite demand is demand for a good that has more than one use, while derived demand means that the demand for one good is derived from the demand for another good.
- Joint supply occurs when the production of one good affects the production of a byproduct produced from the same raw material.

- Elasticity measures the proportionate response or change in a second variable following an initial change in a first variable.
- The four elasticities you need to know are price elasticity of demand, income elasticity of demand, cross elasticity of demand and price elasticity of supply.
- When demand is price elastic, a change in price leads to a more than proportionate change in demand. In this situation the price elasticity of demand is greater than 1 (or unity).
- When demand is price inelastic, a change in price leads to a less than proportionate change in demand. In this situation the price elasticity of demand is less than 1 (or unity).
- When price elasticity of demand equals 1 (or unity), a change in price leads to an exactly proportionate change in demand. In this situation the price elasticity of demand is neither elastic nor inelastic.
- The existence of substitutes is the main determinant of price elasticity of demand.
- With income elasticity of demand, the plus or minus sign of the elasticity statistic tells us whether the good is a normal good or an inferior good.
- With cross elasticity of demand, the plus or minus sign of the elasticity statistic tells us whether the two goods are substitutes or complementary goods in joint demand.

# ■ 3.1.3 Production, costs and revenue

These notes relate to AQA AS specification section 3.1.3 and to parts of A-level specification 4.1.4 and prepare you to answer examination questions on:

- production and productivity
- specialisation, division of labour and exchange
- costs of production
- economies and diseconomies of scale
- average revenue, total revenue and profit

## Essential information

### Production and productivity

It is easy to confuse productivity with production. While closely related, they do not have the same meaning.

**Production** is simply the process by which inputs are converted into outputs. The inputs into the production process are the four factors of production (land, labour, capital and enterprise) which we mentioned earlier and which are listed in Figure 8.

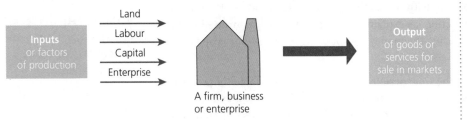

**Figure 8** A firm undertaking production

For most purposes, **productivity** usually means **labour productivity**, which is output per worker. Productivity is a key concept in AS and A-level economics, particularly in macroeconomics, where we look at the UK's productivity gap, which is the difference in productivity levels between the UK and competitor countries.

### Specialisation, division of labour, trade and exchange

If we assume that the capital and land employed by a firm are fixed and cannot be altered, at least in the short run, the only way a firm can increase production is by employing more factors of production such as labour. To start with, as more workers are employed, labour productivity (output per worker) may rise, as the firm benefits from **specialisation** and the **division of labour**, i.e. different workers specialising in different tasks. In the economy as a whole, different firms and industries also specialise in producing different goods and services. This, of course, necessitates **trade** and **exchange**, which take place in the economy's markets.

Nearly 250 years ago, Adam Smith, whom we mentioned on page 19, explained one of the most fundamental of all economic principles: the benefits of specialisation or the

**Production** The process or processes which convert inputs of factor services into outputs.

**Productivity** Output per unit of factor input.

**Labour productivity** Output per unit of labour.

### Knowledge check 9

Explain the difference between production and productivity.

**Specialisation** Workers performing different tasks in the production process.

**Division of labour** Production being divided up into different tasks, each undertaken by workers with different skills.

**Trade** Selling goods or services.

**Exchange** Selling goods or services in return for others (barter) or for money.

division of labour. According to Smith, there are three main reasons why a factory's total output can be increased if workers perform specialist tasks rather than if each worker attempts all the tasks themselves:

- A worker will not need to switch between tasks, so time will be saved.
- More and better machinery or capital can be employed.
- The 'practice makes perfect' argument that workers become more efficient or productive at the task they are doing, the greater the time spent on the specialist task.

On the downside, however, workers might become deskilled and find their jobs uninteresting if all that is involved is constant repetition of a single task, such as attaching wheels to cars passing by on an assembly line. This is a disadvantage of the division of labour.

For specialisation to be economically worthwhile for those taking part in the division of labour, a system of trade and exchange is necessary. This is because workers who completely specialise cannot enjoy a reasonable standard of living if forced to consume only what they produce. The solution is to produce more than what the worker actually needs and then to trade the surplus for that produced by others. Specialisation, the division of labour, trade and exchange are central to the functioning of a modern economy.

## Costs of production

As well as confusing production with productivity, economics students often confuse production and **costs**. Production, as explained on page 23, simply converts inputs into outputs, without considering the money cost of using inputs such as capital and labour.

In the short run, defined as the time period in which at least one factor of production is held fixed, costs of production divide into fixed and variable costs. **Fixed costs** are the costs a firm incurs when hiring or paying for the fixed factors of production. Capital is usually assumed to be a fixed factor of production. **Variable costs**, such as the costs of hiring many types of labour and buying raw materials, change as the firm's level of output changes.

At any level of output, a firm's **total costs** of production can be calculated by adding up the cost of producing each extra unit of output. **Average costs**, by contrast, are total cost divided by total output.

## Economies and diseconomies of scale

Labour productivity increases when a firm benefits from **economies of scale**, but falls if the firm eventually suffers from **diseconomies of scale**. Economies and diseconomies of scale are illustrated in Figure 9, which shows how a firm's average costs of production may change as it increases the size or scale of its operations.

Economies of scale occur when a firm experiences falling average costs as it increases its size and scale and produces more output. If beyond a certain size of firm (point $X$ in Figure 9) average costs begin to rise, diseconomies of scale set in.

**Knowledge check 10**

Explain one benefit of specialisation and the division of labour.

**Knowledge check 11**

It is sometimes said that too much specialisation leads to boredom and worker alienation. Suggest why this might be so.

**Costs** The money a firm has to pay out when hiring the services of the factors of production.

**Fixed costs** The costs of employing the fixed factors of production, such as fixed capital.

**Variable costs** The costs of employing the variable factors of production, such as labour.

**Total costs** The addition of the cost of producing, each extra unit of output.

**Average costs** Total cost divided by total output.

**Economies of scale** Fall in a firm's average costs of production when the firm increases the size and scale of its operations.

**Diseconomies of scale** Increase in a firm's average costs of production when the firm increases the size and scale of its operations.

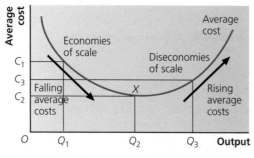

**Figure 9** A firm's average cost curve and economies and diseconomies of scale

There are various types of economy of scale, such as technical and managerial economies. An example of a technical economy of scale is a volume economy. When a warehouse is doubled in dimension, its storage capacity actually increases eightfold. As a result, average storage costs fall as the size or scale of storage capacity increases. However, diseconomies of scale could also set in as storage capacity increases. Stored materials may become mislaid or lost more easily, and the firm owning the warehouse may be tempted to store unnecessary stocks of raw materials or goods awaiting sale. Managerial economies of scale occur because large firms can employ specialist and more highly skilled managers. However, too many managers and a breakdown in communication between them may result in managerial diseconomies of scale.

## Average revenue, total revenue and profit

**Revenue** is the money that a firm earns when selling its output. You must avoid confusing **total revenue** and **average revenue**. Total revenue is all the money a firm earns from selling the total output of a product. It is cumulative. Selling one more unit of a product or good usually causes total revenue to rise. By contrast, at any level of output, average revenue is calculated by dividing total revenue by the size of output.

Likewise, you must not confuse profit and revenue, mistakenly believing that the two terms have the same meaning. **Profit** is the difference between the total sales revenue the firm receives when selling the goods or services it produces and the costs of producing the goods.

Profit = Revenue − Costs

In some circumstances, total costs of production may exceed total sales revenue, in which case there is a loss. Think of a loss as being negative profit.

The revenue a firm earns depends on the competitiveness of the market in which it sells its output. This is discussed in greater detail in the next topic on 'Competitive and concentrated markets'. The main point we shall make is that in highly competitive markets, firms passively accept the ruling market price, which means that total revenue rises by the same amount whenever an extra unit of output is sold and average revenue is constant, however much a firm produces. In concentrated markets, by contrast, total revenue rises at a slower rate than output and average revenue falls when more output is sold.

# Examination skills

The skills most likely to be tested by multiple-choice or data-response questions on production, costs and revenue are as follows:

- Calculating costs, revenue and profit from given data.
- Plotting cost and revenue curves on a graph from given data.
- Relating cost, revenue and profit to a firm's assumed business objective, such as profit maximisation.
- Defining and explaining the meaning of production, specialisation, division of labour and economies and diseconomies of scale.
- Identifying different types of economy or diseconomy of scale.
- Relating specialisation and the division of labour to the role of markets in the economy.
- Relating over-specialisation and diseconomies of scale to the economic performance of a market.

# Examination questions

In AS Paper 1, you should expect up to three of the 20 multiple-choice questions to be set on production, costs and revenue, with at least one question asking for a calculation. In A-level Paper 3, you should expect up to two of the 30 multiple-choice questions (which cover both microeconomics and macroeconomics) to be on production, costs and revenue. Again, a question might require a calculation. See MCQs 5 and 6 for examples. DRQ 2 is a typical A-level question on economies of scale; a similar question could be set at AS, though the number of sub-questions which would follow the extracts would be different.

## Common examination errors

Commonly made mistakes on production and efficiency are:

- confusing production and productivity
- not relating economies of scale to a 'U'-shaped average cost curve
- failure to appreciate how markets facilitate specialisation and the division of labour
- writing over-long descriptive accounts of types of economy of scale
- confusing economies and diseconomies of scale
- failure to understand, correctly apply and illustrate the concept of productive efficiency

## Summary

- Production is the process or set of processes through which inputs are converted into outputs.
- Production should not be confused with productivity.
- Labour productivity is output per worker.
- The inputs into production are called factors of production.
- Land, labour, capital and enterprise, or the entrepreneurial input, are the four factors of production.
- Firms incur production costs when they hire the services of the factors of production.
- Firms earn sales revenue when they sell the output produced by the factors of production.
- The profit firms receive is the difference between total revenue and total costs.

- If total costs exceed total revenue, a firm makes a loss.
- Profit is the entrepreneur's reward for decision making and financial risk taking.
- Specialisation and the division of labour can increase labour productivity.
- Specialisation and the division of labour also lead to trade and exchange.
- Labour productivity rises when a firm benefits from economies of scale but falls if the firm suffers from diseconomies of scale.
- Economies of scale are falling average costs of production when the size or scale of the firm increases.
- Diseconomies of scale are rising average costs of production when the size or scale of the firm increases.

# ■ 3.1.4 Competitive and concentrated markets

These notes relate to AQA AS specification section 3.1.4 and to parts of A-level specification 4.1.5 and prepare you to answer examination questions on:

- market structure
- the objectives of firms
- competitive markets
- monopoly and monopoly power
- the competitive market process

## Essential information

### Market structures

Market structures are most usually defined by the number of firms in the market. However, this leads to other important aspects of market structure. These include competitiveness within the market, which involves the ways in which firms behave and conduct themselves, the extent to which the goods or services being produced are identical or different, and the ways in which barriers to entering the market affect how the market operates.

**Market structures**
The organisation of a market in terms of the number of firms in the market and the ways in which they behave.

**Knowledge check 13**

Explain the difference between a market and a market structure.

Perfect competition and monopoly are the extreme forms of market structure. Along with imperfect competition, which is explained in Student Guide 3, the main features of perfect competition and monopoly are shown in Figure 10.

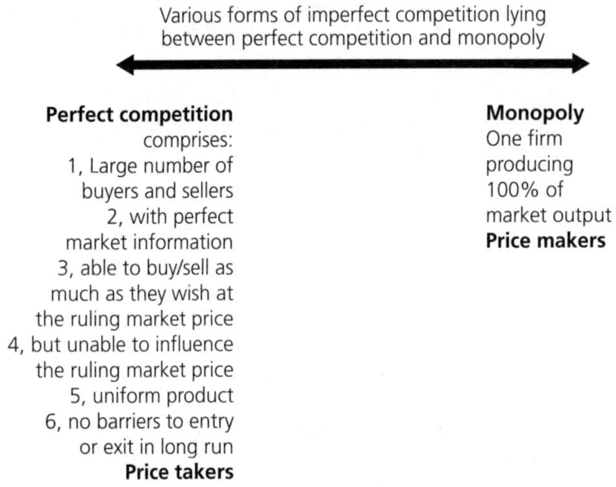

Various forms of imperfect competition lying
between perfect competition and monopoly

⟵──────────────────⟶

**Perfect competition**
comprises:
1, Large number of
buyers and sellers
2, with perfect
market information
3, able to buy/sell as
much as they wish at
the ruling market price
4, but unable to influence
the ruling market price
5, uniform product
6, no barriers to entry
or exit in long run
**Price takers**

**Monopoly**
One firm
producing
100% of
market output
**Price makers**

**Figure 10** Different market structures

Perfect competition is a form of market structure that requires the six conditions listed in Figure 10 to hold. Real-world markets cannot display simultaneously all the conditions necessary for perfect competition. Since any violation of the conditions of perfect competition immediately renders a market imperfectly competitive, the best we can claim for highly competitive real-world markets is that some of them, for instance some markets for commodities such as wheat, approximate to perfect competition.

### Knowledge check 14

List the six conditions of perfect competition.

At the other extreme, as its name implies, a **concentrated market** is a market containing very few firms. Pure monopoly, in which a single firm produces the whole of the output of a market or industry, is the most extreme example of a concentrated market. A pure monopolist faces no competition at all, since there are no other firms to compete against. Usually, however, monopoly is a relative rather than an absolute concept, with a dominant firm such as Apple facing a certain amount of competition in, for example, the smartphone market from firms such as Samsung.

Figure 10 also introduces the distinction between a **price taker** and a **price maker**. A price taker, which is likely to be a highly competitive firm in a market approximating to perfect competition, lacks the market power to influence by its own action the ruling market price. By contrast, a price maker, which has a considerable degree of market power, actively sets the price in the market.

The extent to which a market is competitive or concentrated can be measured with the use of a **concentration ratio**. Concentration ratios provide a good indicator of the degree of monopoly power in a market structure. For example, a four-firm concentration ratio shows the percentage of output in an industry produced by the four largest firms in the industry. A pure monopoly has a one-firm concentration ratio of 100%.

**Perfect competition** A market which displays the six conditions of a large number of buyers and sellers, perfect market information, the ability to buy or sell as much as is desired at the ruling market price, the inability of an individual buyer or seller to influence the market price, a uniform product, and no barriers to entry or exit in the long run.

**Monopoly** When there is only one firm in a market.

**Concentrated market** A market containing very few firms, in the extreme only one firm.

**Price taker** A firm that passively accepts the ruling market price set by market conditions outside its control.

**Price maker** A firm possessing the power to set the price within the market.

**Concentration ratio** Indicates the total market share of a number of leading firms in a market, or the output of those firms as a percentage of total market output.

## The objectives of firms

Economists generally assume that **profit maximisation** is a firm's ultimate business objective. If this is the case, then firms grow because their owners believe that growth leads to higher profits.

Another possible objective is **sales maximisation**, also known as revenue maximisation. Sales or revenue maximisation occurs at the level of output at which the sale of an extra unit of output would yield no extra revenue. Other possible business objectives include **growth maximisation**, **market share maximisation** and **survival**.

Market share maximisation, which tends to accompany growth maximisation, involves increasing the percentage of market output which the firm produces. It often involves a firm trying to increase its market power and monopoly power.

In a highly competitive market, firms may aim simply to survive. In such markets firms are always threatened by new entrants to the market which may steal away their customers.

Finally, it is worth noting that firms may aim to satisfice rather than to maximise. **Satisficing** means achieving a market outcome that is satisfactory for different groups within a firm, such as managers and ordinary workers.

## Competitive markets

As we have noted, Figure 10 lists the conditions or characteristics of a perfectly competitive market. If perfect competition did exist, the market price would be determined as illustrated in Figure 11.

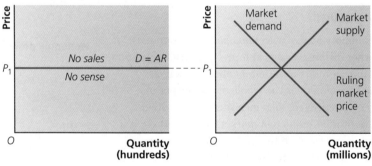

**Figure 11** A firm as a price taker in a perfectly competitive market

A perfectly competitive firm could sell whatever quantity it wished at the market price $P_1$, which is determined by the intersection of the market supply and demand curves in the right-hand panel of Figure 11. However, individual firms would not be able to influence the ruling market price by their independent actions. This results in the fact, illustrated in the left-hand panel of the figure, that each firm is a passive price taker at the ruling market price set by market supply and demand.

The labels 'No sales' and 'No sense' which we have placed in the left-hand panel of Figure 11, respectively above and below the price line $P_1$, help to explain why each firm is a price taker. 'No sales' indicates that if the firm raises its selling price above the ruling market price, customers desert the firm to buy the identical products (perfect

**Knowledge check 15**

What is the difference between profit maximisation and revenue maximisation?

substitutes) available from other firms at the ruling market price. 'No sense' refers to the fact that although a perfectly competitive firm can sell its output below the price $P_1$, doing so is irrational. No extra sales can result, so selling below the ruling market price inevitably reduces both total sales revenue and profit. Such a pricing policy therefore conflicts with the profit-maximising objective that we have assumed firms to have.

Profits are generally lower in highly competitive markets than in those dominated by a few large firms. The reason for this can be explained using the information in Figure 12.

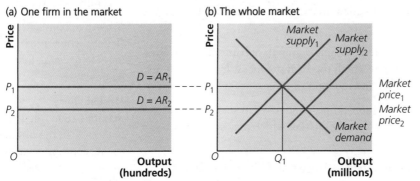

**Figure 12** The entry of new firms reducing the market price in a competitive market

**Exam tip**

Practise drawing diagrams to illustrate market equilibrium in a competitive market.

Suppose that initially the ruling market price is $P_1$, determined in panel (b) of the figure where the market supply curve, *Market supply*$_1$, intersects the *Market demand* curve. The profits made by incumbent firms at this price attract new firms into the market. The market supply curve shifts to the right to *Market supply*$_2$, and the price falls to $P_2$. Because the price has fallen, profits also fall.

## Monopoly and monopoly power

Economics students often confuse **monopoly power** with *monopoly*. In economics, the word 'monopoly' is used in two rather different ways, in terms of a strict definition and a looser definition. The strict definition refers to pure monopoly, which, as Figure 10 states, occurs when a single firm produces the whole of the output of a market. A pure monopolist faces no competition at all, since there are no other firms to compete against. The looser definition refers to a market in which there is a dominant firm, but there are also some other firms in the market. According to this second meaning, monopoly is a relative rather than an absolute concept.

**Monopoly power** The power of a firm to act as a price maker rather than as a price taker.

Since a pure monopoly *is* the industry, the downward-sloping market demand curve is also the demand curve for the monopolist's output. It is also the monopoly's average revenue curve. The fact that it slopes downward affects the monopolist in one of two different ways. If the monopolist is a price maker, choosing to set the price at which the product is sold, the demand curve dictates the maximum output that can be sold at this price. Alternatively, if the monopolist is a quantity setter rather than a price maker, the demand curve dictates the maximum price at which the chosen quantity can be sold. This means that a monopoly cannot set price and quantity independently of each other.

Virtually all firms in the real economy possess a degree of monopoly power, which is the power to act as a price maker rather than as a price taker. Monopoly power is strongest of course when there is only one firm in the market, though the existence of substitute goods produced in other industries reduces monopoly power even in a pure monopoly.

Besides acting as a price maker or exercising the power to set prices, a firm's monopoly power is affected by a number of other factors. These include the existence of barriers to entry, the number of competitors, advertising and the degree of product differentiation. **Entry barriers** prevent new firms entering the market to share in the monopolist's profit both in the long run and in the short run.

Monopoly power is strongest when a firm produces an essential good for which there are no substitutes – or when demand is relatively inelastic. Monopoly may be caused through:

- geographical reasons (e.g. a single grocery store in an isolated village)
- government creating monopolies that are protected from competition by the law (e.g. gambling casinos)
- control of market outlets and raw materials (e.g. breweries and oil companies denying competitors access to the pubs and petrol stations they own)
- using advertising as a barrier to entry: through saturation advertising, large firms can prevent small firms entering the market

Figure 13 illustrates how a monopoly may adversely affect **resource allocation**. In the absence of monopoly, a competitive industry produces output $Q_1$, which is sold at price $P_1$. If a monopoly is formed, the firm restricts output to $Q_2$ and raises the price to $P_2$, thereby exploiting consumers.

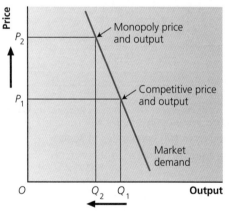

**Figure 13** A monopoly restricting output and raising the price

Monopoly also leads to resource misallocation by:

- restricting consumer choice
- incurring higher costs of production than would be the case in a competitive market. This means the monopoly is productively inefficient (see page 13)
- exercising producer sovereignty at the expense of consumers. This means that unlike in a competitive market where consumer sovereignty rules, the monopoly fails to respond to consumers' wishes, preferring instead an 'easy life'. In effect, this means the 'producer is king' rather than the consumer.

---

**Knowledge check 16**

Distinguish between monopoly and monopoly power.

**Entry barriers** Make it difficult or impossible for new firms to enter a market.

**Exam tip**

Make sure you understand the meaning of entry barriers and are able to give at least two examples.

**Resource allocation** How economic resources are allocated between different industries and eventually, as final goods, to different consumers.

**Knowledge check 17**

What is meant by a misallocation of resources?

**Exam tip**

The concepts of resource allocation and misallocation are often tested by exam questions, both at AS and at A-level.

Under certain circumstances, however, a monopoly may be justified because it improves resource allocation. This can occur for two main reasons:

- By achieving economies of scale, a monopoly can produce at lower average cost and be more productively efficient than smaller firms in a competitive industry. This is illustrated in Figure 14, which shows an industry in which there are economies of scale, but also a limited maximum size to the market. In such a situation there is room in the market for only one firm benefiting to the full from economies of scale: a natural monopoly.
- A monopoly may use its monopoly power and monopoly profit to finance innovation in new products and better ways of making existing products. By contrast, if competitors can instantly copy any successful innovation, a competitive firm may lack the incentive to innovate, and in any case it may lack the profit needed to finance innovation. This argument is used to justify patent legislation, which gives firms an exclusive right to exploit their innovations for a number of years without being exposed to competition.

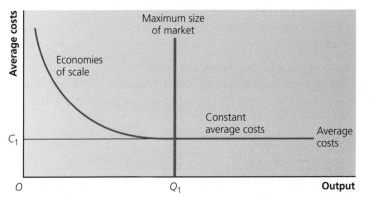

**Figure 14** Monopoly occurs when there is room in the market for only one firm benefiting to the full from economies of scale

Some monopolies are called **natural monopolies**. Natural monopoly occurs when there is room in the market for only one firm benefiting from full economies of scale, which are falls in average costs of production resulting from an increase in the size or scale of a firm.

In the past, **utility industries** such as water, gas, electricity and the telephone industries were natural monopolies. The industries produced a service that was delivered through a distribution network or grid of pipes or cables into millions of separate businesses and homes. Competition in the provision of distribution grids was regarded as wasteful, since it required the duplication of fixed capacity, therefore causing each supplier to incur unnecessarily high fixed costs. In recent years, technical progress, particularly in the telecommunications industry, has weakened and sometimes destroyed the natural monopoly status of the utility industries. Nevertheless, the UK government continues to regulate the utility industries to try to prevent the abuse of monopoly power.

**Exam tip**

In both the AS and A-level exams, questions may require analysis and evaluation of the case against monopoly and the case justifying monopoly.

**Natural monopolies**
The term has two meanings: first, when a country or firm has complete control of a natural resource, and second, when there is room in a market for only one firm benefiting to the full from economies of scale.

**Utility industries**
Provide services such as gas and electricity that are delivered through a distribution network or grid of pipes and cables into millions of separate businesses and homes.

**Knowledge check 18**

Explain why the provision of tap water is a natural monopoly.

## The competitive market process

Firms do not just undertake **price competition**, they also take part in various forms of **quality competition**. Firms strive to improve products and reduce costs. Quality competition also includes the production of reliable 'state-of-the-art', well-designed products, embodying the latest technical progress.

Quality competition is a form of **non-price competition**. This includes the use of persuasive advertising, product differentiation, marketing competition, brand imaging, packaging competition, fashion, style and design, provision of point-of-sale service and after-sale service. The latter, of course, are a part of quality competition.

Forms of price competition that take place in imperfectly competitive markets include special offer pricing, when firms introduce temporary 'special offer' prices on some of the goods they are selling. Supermarket pricing gives many examples of this.

Another form of pricing, used mostly by firms with considerable monopoly power, is limit pricing. With limit pricing, firms already in the market sacrifice short-run profit maximisation in order to maximise long-run profits. By setting low prices, they hope to deter or limit the entry of new firms.

**Predatory pricing** is closely linked to limit pricing. However, predatory pricing is usually illegal because of its anti-competitive effects on the market. Whereas limit pricing deters market entry, successful predatory pricing removes recent entrants to the market. Predatory pricing occurs when an established or incumbent firm deliberately sets prices below costs to force new market entrants out of business. Once the new entrants have left the market, the established firm may decide to restore prices to their previous levels. Both limit pricing and predatory pricing form barriers to market entry.

## Examination skills

The skills most likely to be tested by objective test or data-response questions on competitive and concentrated markets are as follows:

- Identification of different market structures.
- Using concentration ratios to analyse market structures.
- Applying knowledge and understanding of cost and revenue curves to perfect competition and monopoly.
- Analysing how the size of profit is determined in different market structures.
- Showing an understanding of the fact that most competitive markets are not perfectly competitive.
- Appreciating how price taking and price making affect analysis of perfect competition and monopoly.
- Drawing and explaining a diagram to show a monopoly restricting output and raising the price.
- Drawing and explaining a diagram to show a monopoly benefiting from economies of scale.
- Investigating how firms exercise market power.
- Analysis of profit maximisation in competitive and concentrated markets.
- Evaluating market outcomes in different market structures.

**Price competition** When firms reduce prices in order to sell more of a good or service.

**Quality competition** When firms improve the quality of their goods or services in order to sell more of them.

**Non-price competition** When firms use methods other than reducing their prices in order to sell more of a good or service.

**Predatory pricing** Temporarily reducing the price of a good to below average cost to drive new entrants out of the market.

> **Exam tip**
>
> Make sure you can give examples of forms of non-price competition.

> **Knowledge check 19**
>
> Distinguish between price competition and quality competition.

# Examination questions

In AS Paper 1, you should expect up to four of the 20 multiple-choice questions to be set on competitive and concentrated markets, with possibly one question asking for a calculation. In A-level Paper 3, you should expect up to two of the 30 multiple-choice questions (which cover both microeconomics and macroeconomics) to be on competitive and concentrated markets, with a calculation possibly involved. See MCQs 7 and 8 for examples, though neither of the two questions requires a calculation. DRQ 2 is an A-level question relating to market structure. Likewise, DRQ 3 is an AS question on a price war between a new entrant into the taxi market (Uber) and black cabs which have always tried to exercise a degree of monopoly power.

## Common examination errors

Commonly made mistakes on competitive and concentrated markets are:

- inability to perform accurate calculations, for example of concentration ratios
- confusion of perfect competition with imperfect competition
- drawing of inaccurate graphs to illustrate perfect competition and monopoly
- confusion of profit maximisation with other possible business objectives
- failure to distinguish between monopoly and monopoly power
- restricting answers to description when analysis and evaluation are called for
- inability to evaluate the performance of firms in different market structures

## Summary

- Market structures relate to the organisation of a market in terms of the number of firms in the market and the ways in which they behave.
- Market structure can be measured by concentration ratios.
- Perfect competition and pure monopoly are the extreme forms of market structure.
- Perfect competition is a market structure that displays six required conditions.
- These are a large number of buyers and sellers, perfect market information, the ability to buy or sell as much as is desired at the ruling market price, the inability of an individual buyer or seller to influence the market price, a uniform product, and no barriers to entry or exit in the long run.
- Perfectly competitive firms are passive price takers.
- Pure monopoly occurs when there is only one firm in a market.
- Some monopolies are natural monopolies.

- Some markets contain a dominant firm but they are not pure monopolies.
- Firms can exercise monopoly power even though they are not pure monopolies.
- Monopolies are active price makers.
- Barriers to market entry promote monopoly and the exercise of monopoly power.
- The case against monopolies centres on their ability to restrict output so as to raise prices.
- However, monopolies may be justified by their ability to benefit from economies of scale and to be dynamically efficient.
- Economists usually assume that firms in all market structures aim to maximise profit.
- But firms may have other business objectives such as market share and growth maximisation.
- Satisficing is another possibility.
- It is important to distinguish between price competition and forms of non-price competition such as quality competition.

# ■ 3.1.5 The market mechanism, market failure and government intervention in markets

These notes relate to the AQA AS specification section 3.1.5 and parts of the A-level specification 4.1.8, and prepare you to answer examination questions on:

■ how markets and prices allocate resources
■ the meaning of market failure
■ public goods, private goods and quasi-public goods
■ merit and demerit goods
■ market imperfections
■ an inequitable distribution of income and wealth
■ government intervention in markets
■ government failure

## Essential information

### How markets and prices allocate resources

To understand how markets and prices allocate resources in an economy, we must explain the four functions prices perform in markets. These are the:

■ signalling function
■ incentive function
■ rationing function
■ allocative function

In the first place, prices provide information that allows buyers and sellers in a market to plan and coordinate their economic activities. This is the signalling function of prices. The information signalled by changing relative prices then creates incentives for people to alter their economic behaviour. For example, a higher price creates an incentive for firms to supply more of a good or service. By contrast, the rationing function of prices relates to demand rather than to supply: a rising price rations demand for a product.

The rationing function of prices is related to, but not quite the same as, the allocative function of prices. The rationing function distributes scarce goods to those consumers who value them most highly. By contrast, the allocative function directs resources between markets, away from the markets in which prices are too high and in which there is excess supply, towards the markets where there is excess demand and price is too low.

### The meaning of market failure

Market failure occurs whenever markets perform badly or unsatisfactorily. Markets may fail either because they perform inequitably (unfairly or unjustly) or because they perform inefficiently.

■ Markets performing inequitably. Different people have different opinions about what is fair, so the first type of market failure depends on normative views or value judgements.

> **Exam tip**
>
> It is important to recognise that when markets perform well, prices convey accurate information and create suitable incentives to which economic agents can respond. But when one or more of the four functions of prices performs unsatisfactorily, or in extreme cases breaks down completely, market failure occurs.

- Many economists argue that inequalities in the distributions of income and wealth provide a significant example of market failure resulting from markets performing inequitably.
- Markets performing inefficiently. Whenever markets result in productive inefficiency, or when they misallocate resources between competing uses, the second type of market failure occurs.

Market failure also occurs if one or more of the four functions of prices breaks down. When all four functions break down, a market fails to function at all, complete market failure occurs and the result is a missing market. By contrast, if only one of the functions of prices, say the signalling function or the incentive function, breaks down, partial market failure occurs. Prices are either too high or too low, thereby creating the 'wrong' incentives, with the result that a good or service is under-consumed or over-consumed.

## Public goods, private goods and quasi-public goods

Most goods are **private goods**, possessing two important characteristics:

- The owners can exercise private property rights, preventing other people from using the good or consuming its benefits – unless they are prepared to pay a price for the good in the market. This property is called excludability.
- The second characteristic possessed by a private good is rivalry or diminishability: when one person consumes the good, fewer of the benefits are available for other people.

A public good exhibits the opposite characteristics of **non-excludability** and **non-rivalry** or non-diminishability. It is these that lead to market failure. Suppose an entrepreneur builds the lighthouse shown in Figure 15 and then tries to charge each ship benefiting from the service provided, namely the beam of light. As long as the ships pay up, the service can be provided commercially through the market. However, the market is likely to fail because the incentive function of prices breaks down. Because it is impossible to exclude free-riders (ships that benefit without paying), it may be impossible to collect enough revenue to cover costs. If too many ships decide to 'free-ride', profits cannot be made and the incentive to provide the service through the market disappears. The market thus fails to provide a service for which there is an obvious need; hence the case for alternative provision by the government in its public spending programme, or possibly by a charity.

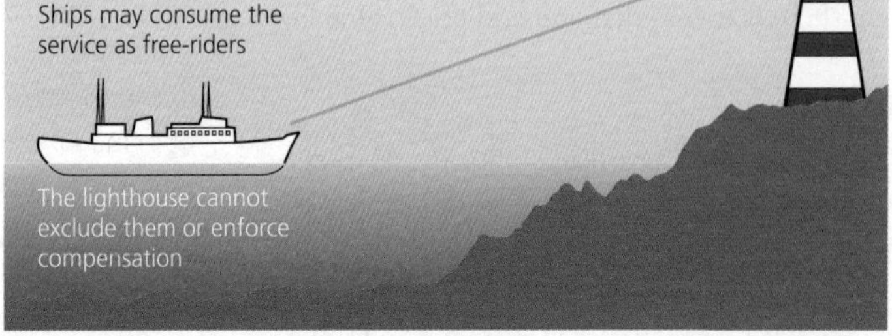

**Private goods** Goods such as apples, which are both excludable and rival.

**Non-excludability** It is impossible to exclude a free-rider.

**Non-rivalry** Consumption by one person does not diminish the quantity of the good available to others.

### Knowledge check 20

Give an example of a person 'free-riding' on another person.

The lighthouse cannot easily collect revenues for the service it provides

The beam of light provided by a lighthouse is a public good

Ships may consume the service as free-riders

The lighthouse cannot exclude them or enforce compensation

**Figure 15** A lighthouse as a public good

### Exam tip

You must not confuse a public good with a government good, which is any good provided by government.

You should distinguish between a **pure public good** and a **quasi-public good**. National defence and police are examples of pure public goods – defined as public goods for which it is impossible to exclude free-riders. However, most public goods (street lighting, roads and lighthouses) are quasi-public goods. Methods can be devised for converting the goods into private goods by excluding free-riders (for example, electronic pricing of road use). Quasi-public goods can be provided by markets, although the second property of non-rivalry or non-diminishability means there is a case for providing all public goods free in order to encourage as much consumption as possible.

A pure public good is an example of market failure resulting from the complete absence of a market – a missing market, which we mentioned earlier. With a pure public good, such as national defence, the market may simply not exist. Assuming there is a need for public goods, some mechanism other than the market mechanism must be used to provide the goods. The usual response is for governments to provide public goods free at the point of use for consumers, with provision paid for collectively through taxation. Another possibility is provision by charities.

## Positive and negative externalities in consumption and production

An **externality** is a special type of public good or public 'bad' that is 'dumped' by those who produce it on to other people (known as third parties) who receive or consume it, whether or not they choose to. Externalities, which exist when there is a divergence between private and social benefits and costs, can be divided into **positive externalities** and **negative externalities**, or external benefits and external costs. A positive externality, or external benefit, is enjoyed by a third party as a result of a market transaction. A negative externality is a cost incurred by third parties as a result of a market transaction.

> ### Exam tip
> Remember that both public goods and externalities provide examples of missing markets.

As with pure public goods such as national defence, the key feature of an externality is that there is no market in which it can be bought or sold. Since they are produced and received outside the market, externalities provide another example of 'missing markets'.

Externalities provide further examples of the free-rider problem. The provider of an external benefit (or positive externality), such as a beautiful view, cannot charge a market price to any willing free-riders who enjoy it, while conversely, the unwilling free-riders who receive or consume external costs (or negative externalities), such as pollution and noise, cannot charge a price to the polluter for the 'bad' they reluctantly receive.

**Pure public good** A good that is always non-excludable and non-rival.

**Quasi-public good** A good that in certain circumstances can be excludable.

### Knowledge check 21

Give an example, other than the ones listed above, of a market providing a quasi-public good.

**Externality** A public good, in the case of an external benefit, or a public 'bad', in the case of an external cost, that is 'dumped' on third parties 'outside the market'.

**Positive externality** A benefit enjoyed by a third party as a result of an economic activity. Also known as an external benefit.

**Negative externality** A cost suffered by a third party as a result of an economic activity. Also known as an external cost.

As well as being divided into external benefits and costs, externalities can be classified according to whether they are generated in consumption or in the course of production. Consider a lady planting a beautiful garden for her private pleasure. Other people walking nearby also enjoy looking at the garden. A positive **consumption externality** has been generated. Contrast this with a positive **production externality**, for example the pleasure gained by passers-by from viewing the blossom in a commercial orchard. In the course of consumption and production, negative externalities are also generated. An example of a negative consumption externality is the displeasure suffered by non-smokers forced to inhale tobacco fumes exhaled by smokers at a bus stop. A negative production externality would be people inhaling diesel fumes emitted by passing lorries on the way to make their deliveries.

## Merit and demerit goods

A **merit good**, such as education or healthcare, is a good or service for which the social benefits of consumption enjoyed by the whole community exceed the private benefits received by the consumer. Consumption by an individual produces positive externalities that benefit the wider community.

Whereas markets may fail to provide any quantity at all of a pure public good, such as defence, they can certainly provide education and healthcare, as the existence of private fee-paying schools and hospitals clearly demonstrates. However, if schools and hospitals are available only through the market at prices unadjusted by subsidy, people (especially the poor) will choose to consume too little of their services. The resulting under-consumption of merit goods represents a misallocation of resources.

As their name suggests, **demerit goods** are the opposite of merit goods. The social costs to the whole community resulting from the consumption of a demerit good, such as tobacco or alcohol, exceed the private costs incurred by the consumer. This is because consumption by an individual produces negative externalities that harm the wider community. The private cost can be measured by the money cost of purchasing the good, together with any health damage suffered by the person consuming the good. But the social costs of consumption include the cost of the negative externalities – for example, the costs of damage and injury inflicted on other people from tobacco smoke, and from road accidents caused by drunken drivers. Thus, if demerit goods are provided only through the market, at prices unadjusted by taxation, people will choose to consume too much of the goods. Again, the over-consumption of demerit goods results in resource misallocation.

Merit goods and demerit goods can possess a further characteristic (besides the divergence between private and social costs and benefits), which leads to their under-consumption or over-consumption. Individuals consuming merit and demerit goods may not act in their own best interest because they consider only short-term utility maximisation rather than long-term utility maximisation. For the individual concerned, the long-term private benefits of consuming a merit good, such as education and healthcare, exceed the short-term private benefits. For example, in a market situation, many people under-purchase healthcare services such as regular dental checks and end up suffering the consequences later in life. People are likely to choose to consume too little of the merit good early in life, and later in life they may wish they had consumed more. This is an example of an **information problem**.

**Consumption externality** A benefit or cost experienced by a third party, generated by the activities of consumers.

**Production externality** A benefit or cost experienced by a third party, generated by the activities of producers.

**Merit good** A good or service such as education, for which the social benefits of consumption exceed the private benefits.

### Knowledge check 22

Distinguish between a merit good and a public good.

**Demerit good** A good or service such as cocaine for which the social costs of consumption exceed the private costs.

### Exam tip

Many students assert that any good that is 'good for you' is a merit good and that any good that is 'bad for you' is a demerit good. These assertions are wrong.

**Information problem** Occurs when people make wrong decisions because they don't possess or they ignore relevant information.

Similarly, with a demerit good such as tobacco, the long-term private costs of consumption can exceed the short-term private costs. A teenage boy or girl who develops a smoking habit may regret later in life the decision to start smoking, particularly if he or she eventually contracts a smoking-related disease. With both merit and demerit goods, many economists argue that an authority outside the individual, such as the state, is a better judge than individuals themselves of what is good for them. The state should thus encourage the consumption of merit goods and discourage the consumption of demerit goods for the individual's own interest, as well as for the wider social interest.

Whether a good is classified as a merit good or a demerit good, or indeed as neither, thus depends crucially on the value judgements of the person making the classification. This is an important example of the distinction between positive and normative statements.

Figures 16 and 17 illustrate how, if demerit goods and merit goods are available in markets at prices respectively unadjusted by taxation or subsidy, too much of the demerit good and too little of the merit good are produced and consumed.

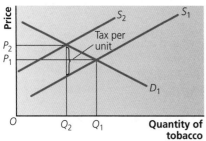
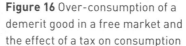

**Figure 16** Over-consumption of a demerit good in a free market and the effect of a tax on consumption

Figure 16 shows too much tobacco being consumed when bought at market prices. At least in the short run, the privately optimal level of tobacco consumption is $Q_1$, located where the market demand curve $D_1$ for tobacco intersects the market supply curve $S_1$. At this level of consumption, the price of a packet of cigarettes is $P_1$. Because smokers generate negative consumption externalities, $Q_1$ is higher than the socially optimal level of consumption, which is $Q_2$. Supply curve $S_1$ depicts the private costs of smoking. However, supply curve $S_2$ shows the social costs of smoking. $Q_2$ is located below the point where $D_1$ intersects $S_2$. Free-market provision therefore leads to over-consumption and hence over-production of tobacco products. In a free market, too many scarce resources are allocated to their production.

The solution could be a tax on the sale of tobacco products, which shifts the market supply curve to $S_2$, thereby raising the price to $P_2$ and reducing consumption to $Q_2$. If the government deems the socially optimal level of consumption of tobacco is zero, a very large tax would be needed to achieve this end. Alternatively, the government might decide to ban the production, sale and consumption of tobacco products. However, as we shall see shortly, both taxation and an outright ban are likely to lead to government failure.

In contrast to a demerit good, consumption of merit goods such as education generates positive externalities which benefit the whole community. As a result, the social benefit of consumption exceeds the private benefit enjoyed by the consumer. If educational services are provided solely through the market, and at market prices, too few people benefit from education. Figure 17 helps to explain why.

**Knowledge check 23**

Is there a case for the state not intervening in the provision of merit and demerit goods?

**Exam tip**

In an exam answer, you can define a merit or a demerit good either in terms of the externalities generated when the good is consumed, or in terms of the information problem associated with the consumption of the good.

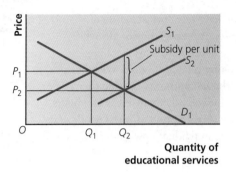

**Figure 17** Under-consumption of a merit good in a free market

In Figure 17, the market supply curve of education is $S_1$. The curve shows the quantity of school places that private schools are prepared to supply at different possible annual prices for education. The market demand curve $D_1$ shows how much education parents are prepared to buy for their children at the different possible prices. In this situation, the market price of education is $P_1$, determined where the market demand and supply curves intersect. At this price, $Q_1$ children are educated.

The price would have to fall to $P_2$ to bring about the socially optimal level of education of $Q_2$, which reflects the positive consumption externalities generated when children are educated. However, in a free market, schools would refuse to reduce the price they charge for education, as this would wipe out their profits. Free-market provision of merit goods therefore leads to under-consumption and hence to their under-production. In a free market, too few scarce resources are allocated to the production and consumption of merit goods. The solution could be a government subsidy granted to schools, which shifts the market supply curve to $S_2$.

## Market imperfections

If you refer back to 'Monopoly and monopoly power' in the section 'Competitive and concentrated markets', it explains how, compared with competitive markets and in pursuit of excess profit, monopolies are likely to restrict market output and raise prices. The result is consumer exploitation. Prices end up being too high, with too few of society's scarce resources being allocated to the market in which the monopoly is producing. However, as this section also explains, sometimes the benefits of monopoly can exceed the costs, in which case there is no market failure.

## An inequitable distribution of income and wealth

We explained at the beginning of this topic, when considering the meaning of market failure, how inequalities in the distribution of income and wealth are regarded by many economists as a market failure in terms of the inequitable functioning of markets. However, economists have different views on whether inequalities in the distributions of **income** and **wealth** should be regarded as market failures.

While there is general agreement that a completely unregulated market economy produces significant inequalities, some economists believe that government intervention to redistribute income and wealth destroys incentives that are vital for a market economy to function efficiently. In their view, such intervention leads to worse problems of government failure, which we discuss shortly.

**Income** Flow of money received.

**Wealth** Stock of assets, including money owned.

### Knowledge check 24

What is the difference between equality and equity?

As a footnote, we shall also mention how the **immobility of labour** may lead to market failure. Occupational and geographical immobility of labour mean that economic resources are not fully utilised in areas of high unemployment, while at the same time economic growth is held back by labour shortages in areas, regions and countries benefiting from full employment. According to free-market theory, the problem can be cured through wage rates rising in areas of labour shortage, such as London and the South East, and falling in areas of labour surplus, such as Northern Ireland. However, in practice, the market mechanism fails to solve the problem and labour shortages and surpluses persist.

## Government intervention in markets

Economists assume that governments intervene in markets to maximise the social welfare of the whole community, but like ordinary consumers and firms, governments face conflicts and trade-offs when trying to achieve their objectives.

At the microeconomic level, governments intervene in markets primarily to try to eliminate, or at least reduce, market failures that are deemed to be occurring, or to prevent the emergence of market failure in the future.

In the case of complete market failure and the missing markets associated with public goods, government intervention replaces the market, with the government providing goods such as roads and defence. There are also missing markets in externalities, for example the negative externality associated with pollution and the positive externality created by people enjoying looking at a beautiful building. In these cases, governments can intervene to discourage production of the negative externality and to encourage property owners to look after their buildings.

By contrast, in the case of partial market failure, where markets *do* function but prices signal the wrong information and create the wrong incentives, government intervention takes two rather different forms:

- As with government response to complete failure, the government may replace or abolish the market (e.g. direct **state provision**, financed out of general taxation, of merit goods such as state education and healthcare, together with the banning of markets in demerit goods, such as heroin and cocaine).
- Alternatively (or possibly in addition), governments try to adjust prices so as to correct or at least reduce the resource misallocation that unregulated or 'free' market forces are responsible for. Price adjustment occurs through the use of indirect taxes, subsidies, maximum price laws (price ceilings) and minimum price laws (price floors).

Figure 18 illustrates the impact of minimum price legislation (a price floor). Price $P_2$ is a minimum legal price or floor price, imposed by the government, below which it is illegal to trade. The national minimum wage in the labour market is an example. In effect, government intervention distorts the price mechanism and prevents the price falling to the equilibrium $P_1$. The market fails to clear and excess supply persists.

**Immobility of labour**
The inability of labour to move from one job to another, either for occupational reasons, e.g. the need for training, or for geographical reasons, e.g. the cost of moving to another part of the country.

### Knowledge check 25

Why is there a missing market in the case of a public good?

**State provision**
Government spending used to finance the provision of a good or service. Government planners decide what is provided.

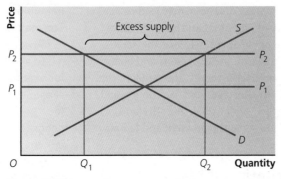

**Figure 18** Effects of government intervention in the market

Regulation, **indirect taxation** and **subsidies** are perhaps the most important policy instruments that governments use to achieve their objectives and to try to correct partial market failure.

Regulation is used in a number of ways, for example to deter monopoly abuse, force people to consume merit goods (e.g. car seat belts), restrict consumption of demerit goods, control the emission of negative externalities and promote positive externalities.

Indirect taxes (and their opposite, subsidies) work in a rather different way. Whereas regulations place boundaries on the way markets can work and thereby constrain how the market functions, indirect taxes and subsidies alter prices within the market. Indirect taxes and subsidies affect the signalling function of prices and the incentives that prices create for consumers and firms. Indirect taxes are commonly used by governments, alongside regulation, to discourage consumption of demerit goods such as tobacco and, illustrating the polluter must pay principle, to punish firms and motorists for the externalities they discharge. Subsidies can be used to encourage consumption of merit goods (e.g. free state education and healthcare) and the production of positive externalities. Permits to pollute, which in effect create a market (in pollution licences) where previously there was no market for pollution, are another way of trying to reduce negative externalities.

## Government failure

Students often assume, rather naively, that when governments intervene in the economy to correct market failure, they always succeed. This is simply not the case. Nowadays economists use the term **government failure** to cover all situations in which government intervention produces an unsatisfactory outcome. Government failures range from the relatively trivial, when intervention is ineffective but where harm is restricted to the cost of resources used up and wasted by the intervention, to cases when intervention produces new and much more serious problems that did not exist before. For example, banning alcohol promotes the growth of illegal and criminal underground markets in which the social costs of consumption may be far worse than in a legal market. As the specification states: 'Students should appreciate that the possibility of government failure means that, even when there is market failure, government intervention will not necessarily improve economic welfare.'

**Indirect taxation**
A tax imposed by the government on producers or firms, some of which is passed on to consumers as a price rise.

**Subsidy** Money given by the government to producers or firms, which use the subsidy to reduce the price that consumers pay.

**Knowledge check 26**

How does a price ceiling affect a market?

**Knowledge check 27**

How can the use of regulation control the emission of negative externalities?

**Knowledge check 28**

Distinguish between the signalling and incentive functions of prices.

**Government failure** Occurs when government intervention in the economy is ineffective, wasteful or damaging.

At this point, it is appropriate to introduce the 'law of unintended consequences'. This 'law', which has become fashionable in recent years, predicts that whenever the government intervenes in the market economy, effects will be unleashed which the policy makers had not foreseen or intended. Sometimes, of course, the unintended effects may be advantageous to the economy, while in other instances they may be harmful but relatively innocuous. In either of these circumstances, government intervention can be justified on the grounds that the social benefits of intervention exceed the social costs and therefore contribute to a net gain in economic welfare. But if government activity, however well intentioned, triggers harmful consequences that are greater than the benefits the government intervention is supposed to promote, then government failure results.

**Exam tip**

Make sure you don't confuse government failure and market failure.

## Examination skills

The skills most likely to be tested by multiple-choice and data-response questions on the market mechanism, market failure and government intervention in markets are:

- Explaining the meaning of market failure.
- Relating the market failure to the breakdown of one or more of the functions of prices.
- Explaining the reasons why market failure occurs in the case of public goods and externalities.
- Explaining how externalities are produced and consumed 'outside the market'.
- Explaining why markets under-supply merit goods and over-supply demerit goods.
- Applying the concept of equity to the analysis of the distributions of income and wealth.
- Explaining how a monopoly may adversely affect resource allocation.
- Drawing and explaining a diagram to show a monopoly restricting output and raising the price.
- Drawing and explaining a diagram to show a monopoly benefiting from economies of scale.
- Evaluating the costs and benefits of monopoly.
- Identifying the many different ways in which governments can intervene in markets.
- Drawing supply and demand diagrams to illustrate the effect of government intervention in markets.
- Relating government intervention to the correction of market failures.
- Appreciating that intervention may not be successful and that problems of government failure may result.

## Examination questions

In AS Paper 1, you should expect up to three of the multiple-choice questions to be set on the market mechanism, market failure and government intervention in markets, with possibly one question asking for a calculation. In A-level Paper 3, you should also expect up to three of the 30 objective test questions (which cover both microeconomics and macroeconomics) to be on the market mechanism, market failure and government intervention in markets, with a calculation possibly involved.

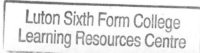

See MCQs 9 and 10 for examples, though neither of the two questions requires a calculation. DRQ 4 is an A-level question on public goods. Likewise, DRQ 5 is an AS question on the production and consumption of cocaine (a demerit good) in a 'repugnant' market. DRQ 6 is an A-level question on income and wealth inequality.

## Common examination errors

Common mistakes on the market mechanism, market failure and government intervention in markets are:

- confusing a public good, such as defence, with a merit good, such as healthcare
- not explaining how and why the market fails in the case of public goods and externalities
- not understanding that markets can and do provide public goods, providing methods are devised for excluding free-riders
- naively arguing that government intervention always succeeds in correcting market failure
- wrongly classifying merit goods such as healthcare and education as public goods because they are often provided by the state in its public spending programme
- failing to understand that markets can produce merit and demerit goods, but they produce the 'wrong' quantity
- assuming that government intervention is always successful and corrects the market failure
- failure to relate intervention in markets to the government's objectives
- describing methods of government intervention when the question asks for evaluation of methods
- inability to use appropriate supply and demand diagrams to illustrate the effect of intervention
- assuming that government intervention is always successful and improves economic welfare
- failure to appreciate the many different ways in which governments can intervene, including state ownership and direct provision of goods and services

## Summary

- Market failure occurs whenever a market or the lack of a market leads to resource misallocation.
- Private goods are excludable and rival whereas public goods are non-excludable and non-rival.
- Public goods divide into pure and quasi-public goods.
- A missing market occurs when a market collapses and fails to function at all.
- A key feature of an externality is that there is no market in which it can be traded.

- Externalities divide into external benefits (or positive externalities) and external costs (or negative externalities).
- Externalities also divide into production externalities and consumption externalities.
- A merit good is a good or service for which the social benefits of consumption enjoyed by the whole community exceed the private benefits received by the consumer.

- A demerit good is the opposite, namely a good or service for which the social costs of consumption suffered by the whole community exceed the private costs the consumer suffers.
- Positive externalities are discharged when a merit good is consumed.
- Negative externalities are discharged when a demerit good is consumed.
- People consuming merit goods (and demerit goods) ignore or downplay information about the long-term private benefits (and costs) that result from consumption. This factor contributes to under-consumption of merit goods and over-consumption of demerit goods.
- Economists have different views on whether inequalities in the distributions of income and wealth should be regarded as market failures.
- Immobility of labour also leads to market failure.

- Governments intervene in markets to maximise the social welfare of the whole community.
- Governments intervene in markets to try to eliminate or reduce market failures and to prevent the emergence of market failure in the future.
- Governments provide public goods because markets fail to provide pure public goods. The government replaces the market.
- Governments replace the market by providing merit goods, though they also subsidise market provision.
- Governments ban production and consumption of some demerit goods, but tax others.
- Governments intervene in markets through regulation, taxes and subsidies.
- Attempts by government to correct market failure may lead to government failure.
- Government failure covers all situations in which government intervention produces an unsatisfactory outcome.

# Questions & Answers

## AS Paper 1 and A-level Paper 1

At AS, Paper 1, 'The operation of markets and market failure', is 1 hour 30 minutes long and has a maximum mark of 70. The exam paper contains two sections, A and B, both of which must be answered. Section A, which accounts for 20 marks (about 29% of the total), comprises 20 compulsory multiple-choice questions, or MCQs. One mark will be awarded for each MCQ answered correctly. Section B accounts for 50 marks (just over 71% of the total) and comprises two data-response questions (DRQs), labelled Context 1 and Context 2, of which you should answer one.

At A-level, Paper 1, 'Markets and market failure', is 2 hours long and has a maximum mark of 80. The exam paper contains two sections, A and B, both of which must be answered. Section A, which accounts for 40 marks (50% of the total), comprises two data-response questions (DRQs), labelled Context 1 and Context 2, of which you should answer one. Section B, which also accounts for 40 marks (50% of the total), contains three essay questions (EQs), of which you should answer one.

## A-level Paper 3

Besides including a case study investigation (coverage of which is included in Student Guides 3 and 4 rather than in this Student Guide), the A-level Paper 3 exam has 30 MCQs, of which roughly half are on microeconomics and roughly half on macroeconomics. The MCQs that follow in this Student Guide are similar to those in both the AS Paper 1 exam and the A-level Paper 3 exam.

## Assessment objectives

Assessment objectives (AOs) are set by the government agency Ofqual and are the same across the AS and A-level economics specifications. The exams measure how students have achieved the following assessment objectives:

- AO1: Demonstrate knowledge of terms/concepts and theories/models to show an understanding of the behaviour of economic agents (consumers, workers and firms) and how they are affected by and respond to economic issues.
- AO2: Apply knowledge and understanding to various economic contexts to show how economic agents are affected by and respond to economic issues.
- AO3: Analyse issues within economics, showing an understanding of their impact on economic agents.
- AO4: Evaluate economic arguments and use qualitative and quantitative evidence to support informed judgements relating to economic issues.

Assessment objectives 1 and 2 are testing 'lower-order' skills, whereas objectives 3 and 4 test 'higher-order' skills. The testing of AO3 and AO4 is slightly more important at A-level than it is at AS.

Weighting of assessment objectives for AS Economics

| Assessment objectives (AOs) | Component weightings (approx. %) | | Overall weighting (approx. %) |
| --- | --- | --- | --- |
| | Paper 1 | Paper 2 | |
| AO1 | 14–16 | 14–16 | 29–31 |
| AO2 | 15–17 | 15–17 | 31–33 |
| AO3 | 10–12 | 10–12 | 21–23 |
| AO4 | 7–9 | 7–9 | 15–17 |
| Overall weighting components | 50 | 50 | 100 |

Weighting of assessment objectives for A-level Economics

| Assessment objectives (AOs) | Component weightings (approx. %) | | | Overall weighting (approx. %) |
| --- | --- | --- | --- | --- |
| | Paper 1 | Paper 2 | Paper 3 | |
| AO1 | 5–8 | 5–8 | 7–10 | 20–23 |
| AO2 | 7–10 | 7–10 | 9–12 | 26–29 |
| AO3 | 9–11 | 9–11 | 6–9 | 26–29 |
| AO4 | 7–10 | 7–10 | 5–8 | 22–25 |
| Overall weighting components | 33.3 | 33.3 | 33.3 | 100 |

# Answering multiple-choice questions

A multiple-choice question contains a 'stem' followed by four possible answers (A, B, C and D), only one of which is correct. The other three possible answers, which are wrong (at least in the context of the question), are called 'distracters'. This means that they are meant to distract students into thinking they are correct, when in fact they are wrong.

There are 20 multiple-choice questions in section A of AS Paper 1, all on microeconomics. The questions test primarily the 'lower-level' skills related to knowledge and understanding in AOs 1 and 2. You must answer all 20 of the questions.

Multiple-choice questions also appear in the A-level exam, but only in Paper 3, 'Economic principles and issues'. There are no MCQs in Paper 1, 'Markets and market failure', or in Paper 2, 'National and international economy'. At A-level, compared with the AS exam papers, rather more of the MCQs test analysis of economic problems and issues, and quantitative skills. The skill of evaluation is *not* tested in the multiple-choice question sections of the exam paper, either at AS or at A-level.

# Answering data-response questions

At both AS and A-level, there are two data-response questions (or context questions in Paper 1). AS and A-level students should only answer one of the two questions. At AS, each of the two data-response questions contains six sub-questions, listed as [21], [22], [23], [24], [25] and [26] for Context 1 and [27], [28], [29], [30], [31] and [32] for Context 2. The mark allocation is 3, 4, 4, 4, 10 and 25 marks for each part of the context or data-response question. The total mark for each data-response question is 50.

# Questions & Answers

At A-level, each of the two data-response questions contains four sub-questions, listed as [01], [02], [03] and [04] for Context 1 and [05], [06], [07] and [08] for Context 2. The mark allocation for the four parts of each question is [01] and [05]: 2 marks, [02] and [06]: 4 marks, [03] and [07]: 9 marks, and [04] and [08]: 25 marks. The total mark for each data-response question is 40.

The layout and structure of the data-response questions will be similar to the six questions that complete this guide. Questions 1, 3 and 5 have been written in the style of AS-level questions, while questions 2, 4 and 6 are in the style of A-level questions. Each question, for both AS and A-level, contains three sets of data, which would be labelled Extract A, Extract B and Extract C for a Context 1 question and Extract D, Extract E and Extract F for a Context 2 question. For both AS and A-level context questions, the first set of data (Extract A or D) is numerical, for example a line graph, a bar graph, a pie graph or a table. The other extracts contain text, in the form of a passage of data, often resembling an extract from a newspaper article.

In both AS and A-level Paper 1, the two data-response questions in the AS exam paper will be structured in exactly the same way and test the same assessment objectives. The questions are supposed to be equally difficult, but in practice almost every student finds one question more attractive than the other. Whichever data-response question you initially favour, don't rush your choice. Careful thought and a sensible final decision are necessary if you are to do yourself full justice. You don't want to realise, 10 minutes into your answer for a Context 2 question, that you can't answer the last part of the question but it is now too late to switch to Context 1.

An 'incline of difficulty' will always be built into the data-response questions, with the earlier parts of each question being the most straightforward. At both AS and A-level, the mark schemes for each part of a data-response or context question start by indicating what an answer must include to earn all the available marks and then what is required to achieve a lower mark. The mark schemes for the fifth part of an AS data-response question and the third part of an A-level data-response question contain three levels of response descriptors, each indicating the skills that must be shown for an answer to meet the requirements of the descriptor. In a similar way, the mark schemes for the sixth part of an AS data-response question and the fourth part of an A-level data-response question contain five descriptor levels.

At both AS and A-level, the final part of each data-response question differs from the earlier parts in three significant ways. First, and most obviously, they carry significantly more marks – 25 – than the earlier parts of the questions. If you time your examination answers unwisely and fail to develop your answer to these 'mini-essay' sub-questions beyond a cursory footnote, you will reduce considerably your chance of achieving a grade A at AS and certainly grade A* at A-level. Second, whereas the earlier parts of the questions should be answered quite briefly, you are expected to write an extended answer of several paragraphs and at least two pages for the final part of a context question. Third, 'higher-level' skills are expected. At both AS and A-level, the examiner marks your script using a levels of response mark scheme containing five levels of response for the final part of the question. The levels of response descriptors for the final part of the questions are the same in every exam and you can find them in the mark scheme for previous examinations. It is vital to familiarise yourself with this mark scheme and to bear it in mind when you practise answering questions.

When deciding how to award marks when mark schemes contain levels of response descriptors, the examiner reads the whole of the answer and then decides which level best fits your answer. When answering the final part of a question (at both AS and A-level), to reach beyond Level 2 into Level 3 your answer must include some reasonable analysis but generally unsupported evaluation. Sound, focused analysis and well-supported evaluation, including a sound concluding paragraph, are required for the highest level, Level 5, to be reached.

# The four key skills

## Knowledge and understanding

With respect to the two lower-order skills of knowledge and understanding, AQA requires you to show an awareness of economic terminology and theories relevant to the Part 1 topics covered in this guide. You must also show awareness of real-world issues, especially those relevant to the UK. At AS, your knowledge and understanding will be tested in the exam by most of the 20 multiple-choice questions in section A of the paper. For section B at AS and section A at A-level, the context questions, you are expected to understand market theory, particularly supply and demand theory and related concepts such as elasticity. You must know about real-world markets, e.g. primary product markets, real-world market failures such as externalities and public goods, and events that have occurred in UK markets in recent years, e.g. in the housing market. Finally, you must understand how events in world markets impact on UK markets, e.g. rising world food prices.

## Application

The penultimate question of each data-response question, both at AS and at A-level, starts with the word 'Explain'. Application requires the selection of an appropriate theory or set of theories from the intellectual toolkit stored in your brain to explain an issue or issues posed by the question. The issue may centre on the causes of an economic problem, or the effects of the problem. You are also required to show application of your knowledge of events that are happening, or that have happened recently, in the economy.

## Analysis

Analysis requires selection of relevant information from the data source(s) and then the use of that information, perhaps as evidence, in your answer. Information in the data is there to provide a prompt or prompts for the answer. You should indicate which bits of the data you are using, mentioning the extract and the line numbers, without at the same time resorting to 'copying out' sentences or numbers from the data. You must also develop the skill to show a 'logical chain of reasoning' with regard to the way in which you are developing an argument.

## Evaluation

Evaluation is the higher-order skill that separates good answers that earn an A or B grade for the data-response question (and an A* grade at A-level) from those that at best reach grade C. Evaluation is also the skill students find most difficult to display.

To evaluate, you need to demonstrate a critical approach to economic models and methods of enquiry, for example the assumption underlying market theory that market forces always tend to eliminate excess demand or excess supply to quickly establish equilibrium. You should also demonstrate the ability to produce reasoned conclusions clearly and concisely and to assess the strengths and weaknesses of economic arguments and limitations of the data in the question.

Competing theories or explanations often lead into evaluation. Evaluation can require you to explain why, in your view, some arguments or lines of reasoning are more important than others. Where appropriate, you must weigh up alternative and competing theories and viewpoints. The assumptions you are making should be stated, considered and sometimes questioned.

You will be required to judge the effects of different types of government intervention in markets, sometimes exploring their possible 'knock-on' and 'feedback' effects induced elsewhere in the economy. Very often, the final parts of a context question ask for consideration of the advantages and disadvantages of, or the costs and benefits of, or the case for versus the case against, a course of action mentioned in the question.

Good evaluation requires you to prioritise the evidence and arguments you introduce into your answer. One way to do this is to explain, when introducing each of the points or arguments you are making, whether in your view it is significant always, significant but only under a particular set of assumptions, or though relevant, rather trivial. When making such points, your answer must go beyond mere assertion, i.e. you must justify your arguments and use evidence.

Finally, there are two different ways of evaluating, but in our view the first way is better than the second. Our preferred way of evaluating is to assess the strengths and weaknesses of each argument as you bring it into your answer. Is it relevant always, or only some of the time when particular assumptions hold? If you organise your answer in this way, make sure that every time you introduce a new argument you start a new paragraph. It is also a good idea to leave a vacant line between paragraphs so that the examiner's eye is drawn to the fact that a new argument is being presented.

The second way to evaluate is to leave it all to the concluding paragraph. At its worst, so-called evaluation presented in the concluding paragraph can boil down merely to a statement such as 'In my view, the case for is therefore stronger than the case against'. Unfortunately such a concluding statement is not evaluation, it is unjustified assertion. Good evaluation in a concluding paragraph must always refer back to arguments used earlier in the answer, making a clear final judgement as to which arguments, if any, are most important.

Perhaps the best approach to organising your answer is to combine the two methods of evaluation, namely evaluate each point as you develop your answer before concluding with a winding-up paragraph that presents an 'overview' or summary of the arguments you believe to be most important.

Finally, it is worth remembering that AQA draws students' attention to a significant distinction between weak and strong evaluation. Weak evaluation consists of little more than assertions, generally unsupported by evidence and by any accompanying analysis. By contrast, strong evaluation uses sound economic analysis to support the conclusions being drawn, plus evidence from the real world.

# A strategy for tackling the examination at AS

1 On opening the examination booklet, turn immediately to section B and spend up to 5 minutes reading both Context 1 and Context 2 questions.

2 Then go back to section A and spend up to 20 minutes answering the 20 MCQs, completing your first run through the questions. While you are doing this, you will be subconsciously thinking about the contexts.

3 Read through both contexts again, paying particular attention to whether you can write a good answer to the last part of each question, which carries the most marks.

4 After careful thought, make your final choice and spend about an hour answering all the parts of Context 1 or 2. When answering each part of your chosen context question, take account of the marks indicated in brackets at the end of each of the sub-parts of the question. Make sure you spend more than half the available time answering the final part of the question.

5 In the last 5 minutes of the examination, complete a second run-through of the MCQs and read your written answers to check for and correct mistakes, including spelling and grammatical errors.

# A strategy for tackling the examination at A-level

1 On opening the examination booklet, skim-read all the data-response and essay questions, but at this stage don't read the data extracts in the context data-response questions.

2 Read the questions in both Context 1 and 2 more fully, paying particular attention to the accessibility of the data and whether you can write a good answer to the final part of each question, the part that carries the most marks.

3 After careful thought, make your final choice and spend about 55 minutes answering all the parts of the context you have chosen. Take account of the marks indicated in brackets for each sub-question when allocating the 55 minutes between each part of the question. Make sure you spend more than half the time answering the final part [03] or [06] of the question.

4 While answering the context questions, you will have been thinking subconsciously about the three essay questions you skim-read earlier. Again, you should choose the essay question primarily on the basis of the relative ease or difficulty of the second part of the three questions.

5 Again, take account of the marks indicated in brackets for each sub-question when allocating the 55 or so minutes between each part of the question. Make sure you spend more than half the time answering the second part of the essay question.

**6** For both your chosen questions, remember to obey the key instruction words at the beginning of each part of the question.

**7** In the last 10 minutes of the examination, read through your written answers to your chosen questions, checking and correcting mistakes, including spelling and grammar errors.

# The exam questions in this guide

This guide includes 16 examination-style questions designed to be a key learning, revision and exam preparation resource. For all students, there are 10 multiple-choice questions.

The guide also includes six data-response questions. Three of these (questions 1, 3 and 5) are AS questions. The other three (2, 4 and 6) are A-level questions. All the DRQs contain three data extracts. AS students could use the A-level questions for revision purposes; likewise the AS questions might provide useful revision for A-level students.

All the questions in this guide can be used 'en bloc' as part of a short trial or mock exam near the end of your course. Alternatively, as you study a topic in the Content Guidance section of this guide, you could refer selectively to particular questions in this section that assess aspects of the topic.

Note: no essay questions and students' answers to essay questions have been included in this guide. Essays count for 50% of total assessment in the A-level Paper 1 and Paper 2 exams, but they are not a part of AS assessment. You will find sample essay questions and grades A, A* and C students' answers in Student Guides 3 and 4, together with advice on how the mark schemes are constructed.

This section of the guide also contains:

- comments on the MCQs, explaining particular features of each question
- correct answers for the MCQs
- comments on the data-response questions
- student answers of grade-A standard (or sometimes A* standard for the A-level questions) and C-grade standard for each DRQ
- comments on each student's answer explaining, where relevant, how the answer could be improved even though, as it stands, it is already a grade A or A* answer. These comments are denoted by the icon **ⓔ**.

# ■ Multiple-choice questions

The ten multiple-choice questions that follow are typical of those set on each of the five topics in the Content Guidance section of this guide. Each MCQ is followed by a short commentary explaining the correct answer and any other matter relevant to avoiding choosing a wrong answer (known as a distracter).

## Question 1 Economic methodology

Which of the following statements provides the best explanation of why data are important in economics?

Data can be used to:

A    Make the subject seem scientific.

B    Test a hypothesis.

C    Obscure important economic relationships.

D    Show the truth.

ⓔ Look out for objective test questions which have words such as 'best' and 'most likely' in the stem of the question. The examiners often put such words into the question when more than one of the possible answers could be correct but one is 'more correct' than the others. In this case, statement B is the only valid statement; A, C and D are largely irrelevant.

## Question 2 The economic problem

Which of the following is a positive economic statement?

A    Education should be made available free for all children.

B    Governments ought to intervene in the economy to correct market failures.

C    A reduction in welfare benefits will increase the supply of labour.

D    Imposing price controls is an unfair method of allocating resources.

ⓔ It is sensible to expect one question in each examination on the distinction between positive and normative statements. A positive statement is a statement of fact or definition (e.g. a metre contains 100 centimetres), or it is an assertion or prediction that may or may not be true, but can be tested to see whether it is true or false. Note the give-away words – 'should', 'ought' and 'unfair' – which indicate the statement of opinion and value judgement in the statements. Statement C can be tested, so is a positive statement. The other three statements are opinions and thus normative.

## Question 3 Supply and demand in a competitive market

Which of the following events might cause the demand curve for chicken meat to shift to the right?

A    A fall in the price of chicken meat.

B    A fall in the price of turkey meat.

C    An outbreak of salmonella infection in chicken meat.

D    The publication of a health report urging people to eat white rather than red meats.

ⓔ This question tests knowledge of the causes of shifts in demand. The publication of the health report specified in the question would alter people's behaviour in favour of eating chicken and turkey (white meats) and away from red meats such as beef and lamb. The demand curve for chicken meat would therefore shift rightward. Although the question does not ask about the demand curves for red meats, the demand curves for beef and lamb would shift to the left.

## Question 4 Elasticity

The table below shows estimates of elasticities of demand for apples and oranges taken from the National Food Survey.

| Elasticity with respect to: | price of apples | price of oranges | income |
|---|---|---|---|
| Apples | −0.29 | −0.07 | +0.32 |
| Oranges | −0.16 | −1.33 | +0.14 |

Which of the following can be concluded from the data?

**A** Apples and oranges are in joint demand.

**B** Apples but not oranges are inferior goods.

**C** The demand for apples is both price inelastic and income inelastic.

**D** The demand for oranges is both price elastic and income elastic.

ⓔ The cross elasticity of demand for apples with respect to the price of oranges is −0.07 while that for oranges with respect to the price of apples is −0.16. Both cross elasticities are negative, so apples and oranges are slight substitutes, rather than in joint demand. Both goods have positive income elasticities of demand (+0.32 and +0.14 respectively) and are therefore normal goods. The price and income elasticities of demand for apples are both less than 1 (ignoring the minus sign for the price elasticity). However, the price elasticity of demand for oranges is elastic. Statements A, B and D are incorrect; statement C is the correct answer.

## Question 5 Cost curves

The schedule below shows the daily costs a firm incurs when it produces different levels of output.

Cost schedule

| Output (units per day) | Total fixed cost (pounds) | Total variable cost (pounds) |
|---|---|---|
| 0 | 20 | 0 |
| 4 | 20 | 25 |
| 9 | 20 | 50 |
| 13 | 20 | 75 |
| 16 | 20 | 100 |
| 18 | 20 | 125 |

In the table on page 54, the average total cost of producing 16 units per day is:

**A** £1.25 **B** £6.25 **C** £7.00 **D** £7.50

*e* The AQA AS and A-level specifications include the following advice: 'Students will be expected to acquire competence in quantitative skills that are relevant to the subject content and be familiar with the various types of statistical and other data which are commonly used by economists. They should be able to make relevant calculations from economic data.' This is an example of a question requiring calculation of an item in a firm's costs of production. It is also an example of a question in which irrelevant information is provided in the data in order to distract you.

## Question 6 Revenue and profit

The schedule below shows the total revenue a firm receives and the total cost of production it incurs when it produces different levels of output.

| Output | Total revenue | Total cost |
|--------|---------------|------------|
| 0 | 0 | £25 |
| 1 | £30 | £49 |
| 2 | £60 | £69 |
| 3 | £90 | £91 |
| 4 | £120 | £117 |
| 5 | £150 | £149 |
| 6 | £180 | £180 |

What is the firm's profit-maximising level of output?

**A** 0

**B** 2

**C** 4

**D** 6

*e* Again this question requires a calculation, in this case of profit. Profit is defined as Total revenue − Total cost. Only two levels of output (4 units and 5 units) yield a positive profit. Outputs zero, 1, 2 and 3 yield a loss, since total cost exceeds total revenue. At output 6 no profit at all is yielded.

## Question 7 A competitive market

In a perfectly competitive industry, there are:

**A** Many buyers and many sellers.

**B** Many sellers, but there might be only one or two buyers.

**C** Many buyers, but there might be only one or two sellers.

**D** Many sellers but one firm that sets the price for the others to follow.

(e) To answer this question correctly, you must draw on the six conditions of perfect competition that are listed in Figure 10, particularly the first condition, that there are a large number of buyers and sellers.

## Question 8 A concentrated market

Price wars are:

**A**    Most likely when there is a monopoly and no substitute products.

**B**    Possible in concentrated markets.

**C**    Inevitable when the government controls the market.

**D**    Never in the interest of consumers.

(e) Even if you know nothing about economics, intelligent interpretation of the first words in each of the four possible answers should lead you to choose the correct answer. Dogmatic statements are likely to be wrong, whereas a statement that something *may* happen is likely to provide the correct answer. Note that when there is only one firm in a market, a price war cannot take place with other market members because there are no firms to compete against.

## Question 9 Merit and demerit goods, income and wealth inequalities and labour immobility

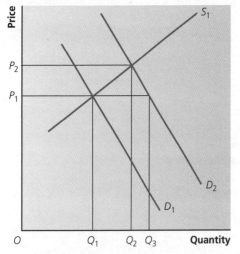

The graph above depicts the market for a merit good such as healthcare. If the government wishes to stabilise the price of healthcare at $P_1$, following a shift to the right of the demand curve from $D_1$ to $D_2$, it should:

**A**    Subsidise healthcare.

**B**    Provide healthcare solely through state spending.

**C**    Impose a minimum price or price floor of $P_1$.

**D**    Take action to eliminate the excess supply of healthcare at price $P_2$.

(e) The graph shows market forces raising the price of healthcare from $P_1$ to $P_2$. Think which of the possible answers will bring the price down once again to $P_1$.

## Question 10 Government intervention in the economy

**Which of the following is an example of government regulation of the economy?**

**A**  The government selling a state-owned industry such as Air Traffic Control to private ownership.

**B**  The government announcing the abolition of rules that restrict the number of commercial radio stations allowed by law to operate.

**C**  The government encouraging the General Medical Council to discipline professionally negligent doctors.

**D**  A legal requirement enforced by local authorities that seat belts be fitted in all coaches and mini-buses.

(e) This question is testing knowledge of methods of government intervention in the market economy. Make sure you don't confuse regulation with deregulation or with other policies of liberalisation such as privatisation.

## Answers to multiple-choice questions

| | |
|---|---|
| **Question 1** | B |
| **Question 2** | C |
| **Question 3** | D |
| **Question 4** | C |
| **Question 5** | D |
| **Question 6** | C |
| **Question 7** | A |
| **Question 8** | B |
| **Question 9** | A |
| **Question 10** | D |

# ■ Data-response questions

## Question 1 The prices of nuts (AS)

### Context 1 Nut prices

Total for this Context: 50 marks

Study Extracts A, B and C and then answer all parts of Context 1 that follow.

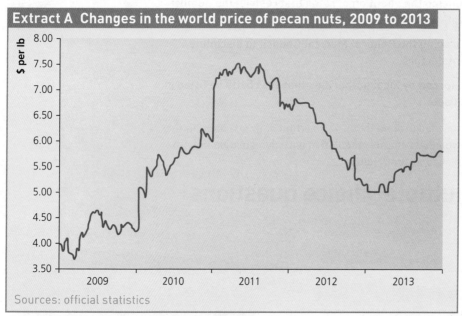

**Extract A  Changes in the world price of pecan nuts, 2009 to 2013**

Sources: official statistics

### Extract B  Rising prices of pecan nuts

High demand, specifically from Asian emerging market economies, is affecting the US nut-growing industry. The USA is the world's main exporter of a variety of nuts. Very often, nut prices are more affected by shifts in supply than by shifts in demand. This has recently been illustrated by what has been going on in the market for pecan nuts. [5]

The US grows 80% of the world supply of pecan nuts. Before 2002, US production was predominantly for domestic consumption, but things then changed. China has now become the world's major consumer of pecan nuts. Pecan nut exports from America to China rose from 1,698m lbs in 2002 to 12,814m lbs in 2009. From the start of 2009 until mid-2011, the price of pecan nuts rose from under $4.00 a pound to $7.50 a pound. [10][15]

The growth of Chinese demand for pecan nuts is explained in part by the rise of the Chinese middle class, whose members have sought a more health-conscious diet. US farmers have responded to the increase in demand by doubling acreage of land they devote to pecan nuts. But because pecan trees take 10 years to mature, nut production is unable to increase immediately. [20]

Pecan nut prices are also affected by the fact that one good harvest is generally followed by a bad harvest. There is a plentiful supply in the 'good harvest' year, but this is followed by reduced supply in the following year. Nevertheless, high production in 2010, which would normally have driven down prices, was accompanied by rising pecan prices, with Chinese consumers driving up demand. The current trend is for demand-side factors to overwhelm supply-side factors, thereby forcing prices up, even in a 'good harvest' year for pecan nut production. [25][30][35]

Source: news reports, January 2014

## Extract C What happened to hazelnut prices in 2014?

Hail storms and frost in March 2014 damaged the hazelnut crop in Turkey, the world's major production country, causing costs to climb by as much as 60%. Around 70% of the world's hazelnut crop is grown near Turkey's Black Sea coast, but 5 the hail storms mean that the 2014 harvest is likely to be heavily hit. By August 2014, speculative buying of Turkey's hazelnut crop had caused global prices to rise by more than 60%.

The world's largest chocolate manufacturing 10 companies are nervously watching the market to decide what to do next. Already faced with the rising price of cocoa, the main ingredient in chocolate bars, chocolatiers are now expecting the cost of hazelnuts, an important ingredient in 15 products such as Ferrero Rocher confectionery, to reach £6,300 per tonne, compared with £3,900 in February.

Ferrero Rocher is the world's biggest purchaser of hazelnuts, buying 25% of world supply. However, 20 the Italian company may not be badly affected by the drop in supply, as it recently purchased Oltan, Turkey's largest hazelnut producer. Other chocolate manufacturers such as Mondelez, the US owner of Cadbury, whose hazelnut-stuffed 25 Whole Nut bar is a best seller, fear that Ferrero Rocher may exploit its monopoly power and deny competitors access to Turkish hazelnuts.

The bad weather in Turkey has coincided with a drought in California which has sent almond 30 prices to a nine-year high. At the same time, cocoa has become more expensive due to a changing market. Cocoa prices are at a three-year high 35 as customers in China and India appear to have developed a sweet tooth.

Source: news reports, August 2014

**[21]** Define the term 'shifts in supply' (Extract B, line 5). [3 marks]

**e** For this part [01] of an AS context question, the mark scheme would be similar to the one below:

| Response | Marks |
|---|---|
| For an acceptable definition such as:<br>A movement of the supply curve to a new position.<br>A supply curve moving its position in response to a change in the conditions of supply. | 3 marks |

If the definition is inaccurate or incomplete, award a maximum of 2 marks which may be broken down, for example, as follows:

| | |
|---|---|
| For an accurate definition of supply<br>For stating that a supply curve can shift to the left<br>For stating that a supply curve can shift to the right | 1 mark for each up to a maximum of 2 |

**[22]** Extract B (lines 12–14) states that in the US pecan exports to China rose from 1,698m lbs in 2002 to 12,814m lbs in 2009. Calculate the percentage change in US exports of pecan nuts to China between 2002 and 2009. [4 marks]

**e** For calculation questions, you will lose a mark if your calculation is accurate but you forget to insert the unit of measurement, in this case a % sign.

**[23]** Using Extract A, identify two significant features of the changes in the world price of pecan nuts between the start of 2009 and the end of 2013. [4 marks]

**e** If only one line of data is presented in Extract A, the question is worded: 'Identify two significant features of...' If there are two lines of data, the wording is likely to be: 'Identify two significant points of comparison between...'

**[24]** Lines 14–16 of Extract B state that from the start of 2009 until mid-2011, the price of pecan nuts rose from under $4.00 a pound to $7.50 a pound. Draw a supply and demand diagram to show the effect of a change in demand or supply conditions on the world price of pecan nuts over this period. [4 marks]

ⓔ All you need do when answering [04] questions is to draw a diagram in the space provided in the answer book.

**[25]** Making use of the information in Extract C, explain two possible reasons for changes in the world price of chocolate bars. [10 marks]

ⓔ Part [05] questions ask for 'explanation', but not for 'evaluation'. You will be wasting time if you try to evaluate the points you are making.

**[26]** Lines 23–28 of Extract C state that other chocolate manufacturers fear that Ferrero Rocher may exploit its monopoly power and deny competitors access to Turkish hazelnuts. Evaluate the view that if Ferrero Rocher exercises its monopoly power, market failure will inevitably occur. [25 marks]

ⓔ Look out for words such as 'inevitably' in the question. If you ignore such a word, your evaluation is going to be limited and the mark for your answer will probably not rise above Level 3 (11–15 marks out of 25).

---

**Student A**

> **[21]** The movement of the whole of a supply curve to a new position, either to the left or right of the original supply curve.

ⓔ **3/3 marks awarded.** An accurate definition of a shift of a supply curve.

> **[22]** The answer is 655%.

ⓔ **4/4 marks awarded.** An accurate calculation with the unit of measurement provided.

> **[23]** The price of pecan nuts ranged between a maximum of just over $7.50 a pound in early summer and early autumn 2011 from a low of about $3.80 a pound at the beginning of the data series in January 2009. A second significant feature was continuing volatility in the price of pecan nuts throughout the data period, for example with the price falling from about $6.25 a pound in October 2010 to $6.00 a pound at the end of December 2010, before rising to $7.00 a pound in the next month in January 2011.

ⓔ **4/4 marks awarded.** Two significant features of the data are identified, with full statistical back-up. Although the answer is written clearly, it would be helpful to the examiner to start a second paragraph for the second feature identified.

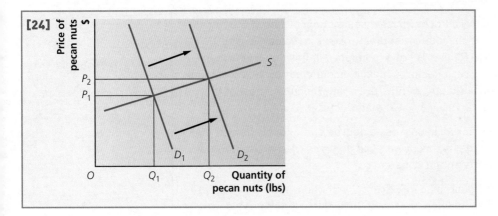

[24]

**e** **3/4 marks awarded.** Although excellent in other respects, the graph loses a mark because prices $P_1$ and $P_2$ do not accurately reflect the two prices mentioned in the extract, $4.00 and $7.50.

[25] Extract C provides three prompts for answering this question. Two of these are (i) the rise in the price of hazelnuts grown in Turkey, and (ii) the rise in the price of almond nuts in California. The third prompt is the statement that the price of cocoa, which I think is the main ingredient in chocolate bars, also increased. However, as Extract C does not explain this was for a supply or demand reason, or possibly both, I shall devote this answer to the hazelnut and almond nut prompts.

Hazelnut prices rose because of bad weather in the form of hail storms along the Black Sea coast of Turkey. This is the main region in the world producing hazelnuts, so this provides the main explanation for the rise in the price of chocolate bars. Because of a rise in the price of a main ingredient, which was also partly due to speculative demand for hazelnuts, the cost of producing chocolate bars increased. The supply curve shifted to the left, up a downward-sloping demand curve, causing the price of chocolate bars to increase (or at least those bars containing hazelnuts).

The same sequence of events took place in the case of chocolate bars containing almond nuts. However, in this case, the triggering event was the effect of drought affecting the almond nut harvest in California, a main production region for almond nuts.

**e** **10/10 marks awarded.** The answer identifies and explains two valid reasons, and indeed mentions a third reason. A graph showing a leftward shift of the supply curve of chocolate bars would have picked up marks, but enough had been done for full marks anyway.

**[26]** The data say that Ferrero Rocher possesses monopoly power, but because there are lots of other chocolate manufacturers, e.g. Mars, we can conclude that Ferrero Rocher is not a monopoly, defined as one firm in a market. And while Ferrero Rocher's main chocolate bar product contains hazelnuts, I don't think that these nuts are an ingredient in most of the chocolate bars manufactured by rival manufacturers such as Cadbury.

Virtually all firms in the world possess a degree of monopoly power; the questions are: how great is this power, and do firms wish to use it to the detriment of rival firms and/or consumers?

The monopoly power described in Extract C is that possessed by Ferrero Rocher, through its acquisition of a major Turkish hazelnut grower. This acquisition gives Ferrero Rocher the power to prevent rival chocolate manufacturers from buying hazelnuts from the company it now owns. Alternatively, Ferrero Rocher could exercise its power by charging its rivals an artificially high price for hazelnuts. But even if Ferrero Rocher wishes to use this monopoly power, its ability to do so will diminish in future years. High hazelnut prices may cause other countries with suitable climates to start to grow hazelnuts, and also in future years there may be very good harvests in Turkey.

A key word in the question is 'inevitably'. Ferrero Rocher may not exercise its monopoly power. The company may in fact allow the hazelnut company it now owns to sell nuts to its competitors, and even if it does try to exploit its monopoly power, for the reasons I have suggested, its exercise of monopoly power may be ineffective. From the evidence in the data, we cannot deduce that monopoly inevitably leads to market failure.

**16/25 marks awarded.** This answer is well written and contains good content. There are two reasons, however, why it has been placed no higher than the bottom of Level 4, 16–20 marks (sound, focused analysis and some evaluation). Most importantly, apart from a cursory mention in the last sentence, there is no discussion of 'market failure', a key concept in the question. The second reason is the lack of a diagram to explain monopoly power.

Total score: 40/50 marks = Grade A

**Student B**

**[21]** A shift of supply is a movement along a supply curve.

**0/3 marks awarded.** The student has confused a movement along a supply curve with a shift of the curve.

**[22]** 655.

**e** 3/4 marks awarded. Although the number is correct, the omission of a % sign means a mark has been dropped.

> **[23]** A first significant feature is that the price of pecan nuts was $6.00 a lb at the beginning of 2011. A second significant feature is that the price of pecan nuts rose over the whole period shown by the data, from just under $4.00 at the beginning of 2009 to $5.50 at the end of 2013.

**e** 2/4 marks awarded. The second point identified is significant and picks up both the available marks (1 mark for identification, the second mark for relevant statistical back-up). However, the first point identified is not significant (a random month taken in isolation) and earns no marks.

> **[24]** Following a shift of the demand curve to the right, the price of pecan nuts rises from $4.00 a pound to $7.50 a pound.
>
>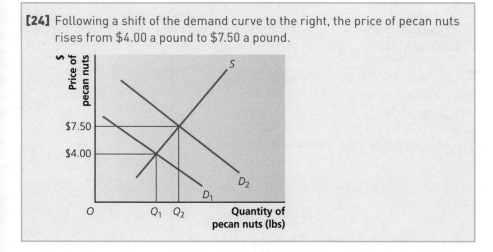

**e** 4/4 marks awarded. An accurate and correctly labelled diagram earns all 4 marks.

> **[25]** Cocoa is the main ingredient in chocolate. As Extract C states, 'cocoa prices are at a three-year high as customers in China and India appear to have developed a sweet tooth'. Almonds are also an ingredient in certain types of chocolate. Again, as Extract C states: 'The bad weather in Turkey has coincided with a drought in California which has sent almond prices to a nine-year high.'

**e** 6/10 marks awarded. The student loses 2 marks for each of the explanations. This is because the explanations rely too much on quoting the data, without further development of what is already in the extracts.

**[26]** Market failure occurs when markets perform badly or unsatisfactorily. There are many types of market failure, including public goods, merit goods, and negative externalities such as pollution. Monopoly is also often said to be a market failure. The reason why is illustrated in the diagram below:

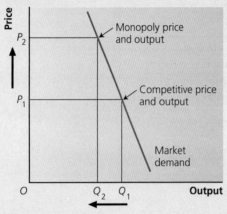

The diagram shows a monopoly deliberately restricting the output it produces so as to raise the good's price. This shows the monopoly exploiting its consumers. As the firm is a monopoly, the consumers are stuck with the monopoly, which adopts a 'take it or leave it' attitude to its customers.

The monopoly power being exercised by Ferrero Rocher stems from it buying a major Turkish firm that grows hazelnuts. It would exercise monopoly power if it prevented its competitor chocolate manufacturers from buying hazelnuts from the supplier it owns. However, the fact that Ferrero Rocher does have competitors, namely other chocolate manufacturers, means it is not a pure monopoly. Because Ferrero Rocher possesses a fair degree of monopoly power, it is likely to try to exploit its position in the market.

ⓔ **12/25 marks awarded.** The answer starts well, with good analysis of how monopoly can lead to market failure. However, it is insufficiently addressed to 'monopoly power' as distinct from 'monopoly'. Having identified how Ferrero Rocher can exercise its market power, the answer also gives a rather limp conclusion, which is not properly justified. In addition, it fails to take heed of the word 'inevitably' in the question. The answer reaches Level 3 (11–15 marks) in the mark scheme, displaying 'reasonable analysis but generally unsupported evaluation'.

ⓔ **Total score: 27/50 marks = high Grade C**

# Question 2 Economies of scale and the division of labour (A-level)

## Context 1

Total for this Context: 40 marks

Study Extracts A, B and C and then answer all parts of the question that follow.

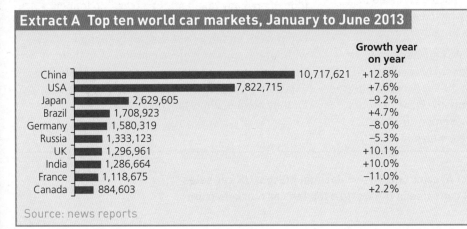

**Extract A  Top ten world car markets, January to June 2013**

| | | Growth year on year |
|---|---|---|
| China | 10,717,621 | +12.8% |
| USA | 7,822,715 | +7.6% |
| Japan | 2,629,605 | −9.2% |
| Brazil | 1,708,923 | +4.7% |
| Germany | 1,580,319 | −8.0% |
| Russia | 1,333,123 | −5.3% |
| UK | 1,296,961 | +10.1% |
| India | 1,286,664 | +10.0% |
| France | 1,118,675 | −11.0% |
| Canada | 884,603 | +2.2% |

Source: news reports

**Extract B  Economies of scale and the mass production of cars**

Since the development of the Model T Ford car in the first decade of the twentieth century, economies of scale have been of great importance in the automobile industry. However, while diseconomies of scale seldom occur in the car industry, globalisation (the increasing integration of national economies throughout the world) is making most car manufacturers vulnerable to competition from rivals in other countries who also benefit from economies of scale. In today's global car industry, a mass-producing car company must produce millions of vehicles a year, or face going out of business.

The 30 or so leading global car manufacturers divide into two categories, with about 15 firms in each category. Each of the members of the top category produces millions of cars a year and enjoys substantial economies of scale.

By contrast, each of the firms in the lower division produces fewer than a million cars a year. Lacking sufficient economies of scale, the smaller mass-producing companies are below the productively efficient size and suffer a significant cost disadvantage when compared with their larger rivals. Before it went out of business in 2005, the UK's MG Rover Group was in the lower division of leading world mass producers. Its relatively small size meant Rover could not compete with industry giants such as Toyota.

Source: adapted from news sources, 2014

# Questions & Answers

## Extract C Economies of scale and monopoly

Economies of scale bring about many benefits. They allow firms to make use of the division of labour and to increase productive efficiency and labour productivity. However, economies of scale can also lead to significant disadvantages. In the first place, economies of scale can lead to the growth of monopoly in which dominant firms exploit not only consumers but other firms also.

Achieving economies of scale can also have adverse effects on employees. This is well illustrated by the growth in the early twentieth century of the Ford car company. Prior to Henry Ford's introduction of the assembly line, cars were produced by craftsmen, who had to be highly skilled and knowledgeable about automobile technology. Many craftsmen were capable of building an entire car by themselves.

Then Ford came along and started to build cars using the assembly line process. Workers, or indeed anybody taken off the street, no longer had to know much or anything about cars. They could work on the wheel assembly section without having ever seen a car engine in their lives. As long as workers can turn the screw when a part of a car is in front of them, that's all they need to know and do.

Source: adapted from news sources, 2014

**[01]** Using the data in Extract A, calculate, to two decimal places, UK car sales as a percentage of total car sales in the world's top ten car markets from January to June 2013. [2 marks]

**ⓔ** The wording of a part [01] question at A-level involves the same sort of calculation as is involved in part [02] of an AS question (see question on page 60). However, only 2 marks are available at A-level, compared with 4 marks at AS.

**[02]** Explain whether the data in Extract A suggest that car sales are growing fastest in emerging market countries. [4 marks]

**ⓔ** The instruction to 'explain' is at the beginning of part [02] and [03] questions at A-level. Note that as a part [02] question carries fewer marks (4 marks compared with 9 marks), the answer should be shorter than for the question that follows.

**[03]** Extract B (lines 2–5) states that 'economies of scale have been of great importance in the automobile industry' and that 'diseconomies of scale seldom occur in the car industry'. With the help of a diagram to illustrate economies and diseconomies of scale, explain these statements. [9 marks]

**ⓔ** To reach the highest level in the mark scheme (7–9 marks), a diagram must be included in the answer to part [03] questions at A-level.

**[04]** Do you agree that economies of scale always lead to monopoly and that monopolies caused by economies of scale are generally good for the economy? Justify your answer. [25 marks]

**ⓔ** Part [04] questions require evaluation in the answers. When you are asked to agree or disagree with an assertion stated in the question, it is generally not wise to agree completely (or to disagree completely) with the assertion, but to argue, and then to justify your argument, that 'it all depends' on the assumptions you are making. One set of assumptions might lead to agreement, but alternative assumptions could lead to the opposite result.

**[01]** The answer is 1,296,961/30,379,209, which is 4.27%.

🅔 **2/2 marks awarded.** This answer earns both of the available marks. The calculation is accurate and the answer is presented to two decimal points. The calculated answer is 4.2692388%, but rounded to two decimal points this becomes 4.27%.

**[02]** An emerging market economy has some of the characteristics of a developed industrialised economy though it is not as yet fully developed. Growth in car sales year on year in 2013 was 12.8% in China and 10.0% in India, with both countries generally classified as newly emerging market economies. Of the other so-called 'BRIC' emerging market economies, Brazil enjoyed 4.7% growth in sales, but sales in Russia fell by 5.3%. However, car sales in the UK, a developed country, increased rapidly, by 10.1%, but sales in other developed countries such as Japan and France fell. Overall, the statistics are quite mixed, but the two highest percentage increases were in emerging market economies.

🅔 **4/4 marks awarded.** Without unnecessarily quoting the growth or fall in sales of all the 'top ten' countries, the answer addresses the question, gives a good overview and uses statistics accurately.

**[03]** Economies and diseconomies of scale can be illustrated on a firm's long-run average cost curve, similar to the diagram later in my answer. In the case of a 'U'-shaped long run average cost curve, economies of scale are benefited from moving along the downward-sloping section of the average cost curve, until the optimal level of output is reached at the lowest point on the curve. After that point, diseconomies of scale set in and long-run average costs rise.

Mass-producing car manufacturers enjoy substantial economies of scale. If they don't achieve these economies, car manufacturers are likely to go bankrupt, as shown by the closure of Rover in the UK in 2005. In a global market in which substantial over-production occurs, firms such as Peugeot in France have been tottering on the edge of bankruptcy. The floor pans on which cars are built provide an example of economies of scale. The VW Group, which is Germany's largest car producer, uses the same floor pan in the VW Passat, the Audi A4 and in cars it manufactures in the Czech Republic and in Spain. The cost of developing the floor pan is spread across all these different VW brands.

Diseconomies of scale can occur in car manufacturing, especially managerial diseconomies of scale, when too many managers are employed. When car companies are located close together, external diseconomies of scale can occur, for example when car manufacturers compete for scarce labour.

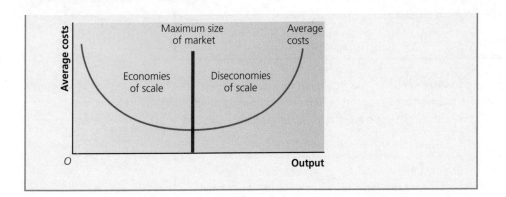

**ⓔ 7/9 marks awarded.** The first two paragraphs and the diagram were on line for full marks, but the third paragraph, which addresses the second statement in the question, lacks development and analysis. This is why the answer has been placed at the bottom of the highest Level 3 (7–9 marks).

**[04]** In the case of natural monopoly, economies of scale do lead to monopoly. This follows from the definition of a natural monopoly, which is a market or industry in which there is room in the market for only one firm benefiting to the full from economies of scale. Such a situation is illustrated in the diagram below.

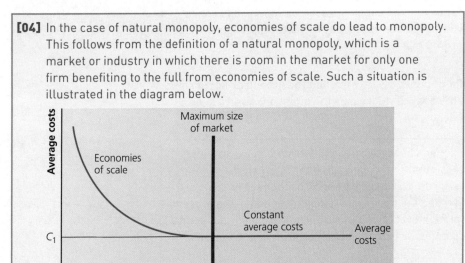

However, if we remove the market size constraint, there can be room in the market for more than one firm benefiting to the full from economies of scale. Economies of scale can justify monopoly but economies of scale don't always lead to monopoly. It is also worth noting that when there is only one firm in an industry in a country, there appears to be a monopoly. However, if the market is open to international trade, competition from imports may considerably reduce the monopoly power of the so-called monopoly.

Monopolies are generally good for the economy if the lower average costs created by economies of scale are passed on to consumers in the form of lower prices. Such monopolies can also be good if the monopolies use their profits to finance research and development (R&D) of new products and more productively efficient ways of making existing products.

However, even when a monopoly is formed as a result of the 'virtuous' pursuit of economies of scale, there is always the danger that, once formed, the monopoly could use its market power to exploit consumers. It might restrict output and hike up the price; it may refuse to innovate, and it may also restrict consumer choice.

For this reason, governments often regulate monopolies to try to make sure that they continue to behave in a virtuous way and are not tempted to slip into monopoly abuse. But if regulation is non-existent or ineffective (an example of government failure), monopoly may not generally be good for the economy, even when substantial economies of scale are enjoyed by the monopoly. A recent case has been the British Airport Authority, which used to have monopoly control over the three main London airports. Although BAA benefits from substantial economies of scale, it was criticised for exploiting passengers, for example by creating too many luxury stores at the airports it owns, at the expense of customer toilets and seats for passengers waiting to fly.

In conclusion, my answer to both parts of the question is that economies of scale don't always lead to monopoly, but when they do, whether the monopoly is good for the economy depends on the monopoly's behaviour or conduct, and on whether effective regulatory constraints are in place to force the monopoly to behave itself.

ⓔ **23/25 marks awarded.** This is an excellent answer that certainly reaches Level 4 in the generic AQA mark scheme for part [04] questions. In fact, because of the good evaluation and reasonable conclusion shown in the answer, it is placed in the middle of Level 5. The student uses the case of natural monopoly to show how economies of scale can lead to monopoly. S(he) then uses the prompt provided by the car industry in Extracts B and C when arguing that large size does not inevitably lead to monopoly. S(he) continues by arguing that a monopoly may behave virtuously, but the danger that it will start to abuse its power justifies regulation. A second example (BAA) is then chosen from the student's general knowledge. Throughout, the answer contains analysis and evaluation.

ⓔ **Total score: 36/40 marks = Grade A\***

## Student B

**[01]** The answer is 4.

ⓔ **0/2 marks awarded.** The student loses a mark by ignoring the instruction to calculate the answer to two decimal places and loses the second mark by failing to include a % sign. Hence, no marks.

**[02]** An emerging market economy is an economy that is emerging from recession or depression. The UK was in this position in 2009 and 2010. Extract A shows that car sales were growing second fastest (behind China) in 2013, when the UK was still emerging from recession, so this supports the argument that car sales were growing fast, though not necessarily fastest in emerging market economies.

ⓔ **0/4 marks awarded.** Again zero marks, but in this case because the student completely misunderstood the question. S(he) took a wild guess with regard to the meaning of an emerging market economy, but unfortunately the guess was wrong.

**[03]** Economies and diseconomies of scale are illustrated in the following diagram. Economies of scale are shown on the left-hand part of the diagram when the firm's average costs of production are falling, with diseconomies of scale on the right-hand part when average costs are rising.

The reason why economies of scale occur lies in the law of diminishing returns. The car industry in particular is likely to benefit from this law, hence the first part of the statement in the question is correct. However, as more and more workers are added to the firm's fixed capital, diminishing returns to labour must eventually set in, so diseconomies of scale eventually occur. This means the second statement is wrong.

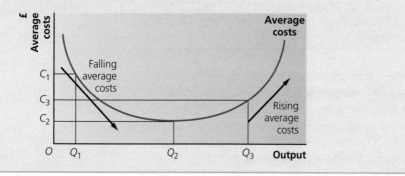

ⓔ **2/9 marks awarded.** The only marks picked up by the answer are for the diagram. Even here, the diagram is not completely correct. It refers to average costs (falling and then rising), without indicating that these are long-run average costs. It is clear from the written answer that the student does not understand the difference between short-run and long-run costs of production.

**[04]** Monopoly occurs when there is only one firm in a market. Strictly, this is 'pure' monopoly, which is very rare. In the UK, the Royal Mail under state ownership used to be a pure monopoly, at least for letter delivery, but since privatisation, this is no longer the case.

Rather more industries are 'monopolistic' and not pure monopolies. In this case, there is a dominant firm which faces some competition from rival firms. A good example is the computer software industry, where Microsoft, the dominant firm, has to compete with Apple, Linux and others.

Monopolies and highly concentrated markets can be good or bad for consumers. A 'good' monopoly is one which benefits from economies of scale and passes the resulting low costs on to consumers as low prices. 'Good' monopolies often come into existence almost by accident. By achieving economies of scale in a market where there isn't room for more than one firm to benefit to the full from economies of scale, the most productively efficient firm drives its competitors out of the market. Monopoly results, but providing the low-cost surviving firm behaves in a benign way and does not exploit consumers, the end result is 'good for the economy'.

A 'bad' monopoly is illustrated in the diagram that follows, which shows a cartel or price ring. Strictly, a cartel contains several firms and is not a pure monopoly, but by forming a price ring, the members of the cartel act as if they are a single firm. Cartel agreements enable inefficient firms to stay in business, while other more efficient members of the price ring enjoy the profit they exploit from consumers. By protecting the inefficient and enabling firms to enjoy an easy life protected from competition, cartels display the disadvantages of monopoly (high prices and restriction of choice). However, this is without the benefits that monopoly can sometimes bring, namely economies of scale and improvements in productive efficiency.

This is because all the members of the cartel (firms A to E in the diagram) set a price sufficiently high to enable the highest cost firm (firm E) to survive. Since firms A to D produce at lower costs, the high price they charge means that they must be making excessive profits. This outcome is bad for the economy, so cartels are generally illegal.

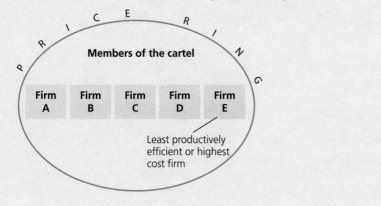

**ⓔ** **20/25 marks awarded.** Perhaps surprisingly, given the poor quality of the earlier answers, this answer is good, reaching the top of Level 4 (16–20 marks), meeting the level descriptor: sound, focused analysis and some supported evaluation. The answer displays much more knowledge of monopoly than did the earlier answers of economies of scale. Economies of scale are mentioned in the answer, but in a relevant way and without mistakes. The main part of the answer addresses the issue posed by the question, but the answer fails to achieve Level 5 because it ends rather abruptly, without a 'rounding up' conclusion.

**ⓔ** **Total score: 22/40 marks = Grade C**

# Question 3 Taxi price wars (AS)

## Context 1

Total for this Context: 50 marks

Study Extracts A, B and C and then answer all parts of Context 1 that follow.

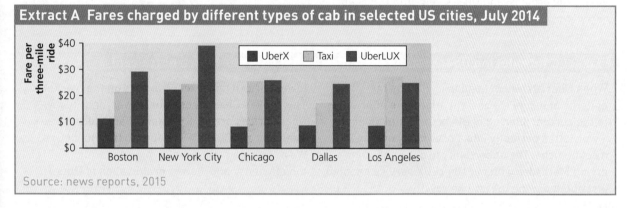

### Extract A  Fares charged by different types of cab in selected US cities, July 2014

Source: news reports, 2015

### Extract B  The entry of Uber into the London cab market

Until quite recently, the London taxi market, in which cabs could be hailed or flagged down in the street, was dominated by Black Cabs or conventional taxis. Entry into the taxi driving profession was strictly limited by the needs, first to spend several years gaining the 'knowledge' of all the streets in the centre of the country's capital city, and second to be granted a cab-driver's licence. The regulatory authorities deliberately kept Black Cab drivers' licences in short supply. 10

Competition with conventional taxis first emerged from minicabs, but they had to be pre-booked by phoning or visiting a minicab company's office and then hoping that the car would show up. But a new form of competition has now emerged 15 which threatens to destroy the Black Cab market. Passengers are no longer subject to the availability of a Black Cab or a pre-booked minicab. They can now make use of a smartphone app that essentially puts a cab in their pocket whenever 20 they need one, in any major city in the world.

By reducing barriers to labour market entry, smartphone technology is destroying the monopoly power of Black Cab drivers. Since the launch of the Uber app in 2009, there has been a massive 25 power shift in the cab market. Uber is a web-based cab booking service accessed via smartphones. The service connects passengers with vetted, private drivers who pick up their customers within minutes and take them to where they want to 30 go. When the booking is made, the passenger's location is pinpointed with the GPS on their phone. The passenger chooses the kind of car they need, checks the estimated price of the journey, and is then told how long they will need to wait for their 35 car to arrive.

Uber has been established in America for much longer than it has been operating in London, where it is a relatively recent arrival. Total weekly rides in a typical December week in 2013 40 were: New York 140,000, Washington DC 110,000, San Francisco 170,000, Chicago 125,000, Los Angeles 120,000 and London 18,000.

Uber, which is now the world's largest cab firm, owns no cars. Uber is an example of a company 45 that controls the interface between the consumer and the provider of the goods or services, which puts it into an incredibly strong position. Uber carries none of the costs of providing cabs for hire but takes a cut from the millions of consumers that buy from them. The interface is where the profit is, and Uber's self-employed cab 50 drivers benefit from this situation. Although they earn less per hour than Black Cab drivers, their total pay is higher because they spend more time 55 on the road picking up earnings and less time off the road waiting for customers.

Source: news reports, June 2015

### Extract C Introducing UberX: same Uber quality but cheaper than a black cab!

When Uber arrived in London in 2013 as the epitome of luxury – a chic yet affordable alternative to the current offering of Black Cabs and minicabs – we slotted perfectly into a previously untapped market niche. The opportunity to get a chauffeur- 5 driven Mercedes with our UberLUX service enabled just about anyone to ride like royalty.

Now that we've mastered the art of elegance on demand, we're celebrating our first anniversary in London by introducing UberX, which offers the 10 quality and convenience of Uber with arguably the lowest priced non-executive cars on the market. This makes Uber accessible to everyone! Today, UberX prices are 40% cheaper than Addison Lee's minicabs and 30–50% cheaper than a Black Cab. 15 We're merging the value of minicabs with the efficiency and instant gratification of Uber.

Source: Uber press release, August 2014

Note: UberX is the Uber company's basic cab service. UberLUX is the Uber company's limousine-style cab service.

**[21]** Define the term 'market niche' (Extract C, line 5). [3 marks]

ⓔ To make sure you earn all of the available 3 marks, make sure you define both words in the term — 'market' and 'niche'.

**[22]** Paragraph 4 in Extract B provides information about total passenger rides in Uber cabs in six cities in a typical week in December 2013. Calculate the median number of weekly rides for the six cities. [4 marks]

ⓔ Make sure you don't confuse the 'median' number with another measure of the average, the 'mean' number.

**[23]** Identify two significant points of comparison between the fares charged by different types of cab in the cities shown in Extract A. [4 marks]

ⓔ You must make sure that your chosen points of comparison are 'significant' and not trivial.

**[24]** Lines 9–10 of Extract B state that the regulatory authorities deliberately kept Black Cab drivers' licences in short supply. Draw an appropriate diagram to show the possible effect of this decision on the supply of Black Cabs in London. [4 marks]

ⓔ For questions on markets, an 'appropriate' diagram is usually a supply and demand diagram, but think carefully whether you need a demand curve in your diagram.

**[25]** Making use of the information in the extracts, explain how the entry of Uber into the cab market may affect the fares charged by other types of cab.

[10 marks]

ⓔ The command word 'explain' means that this question is primarily testing economic analysis.

**[26]** Evaluate the costs and benefits of Uber's entry into the cab market.

[25 marks]

ⓔ Make sure you first identify, and then evaluate, both the costs and the benefits.

| Student A |
| --- |

**[21]** A market is where buyers and sellers meet to voluntarily exchange products, normally for money. A niche is a place suitable to a particular product or person. Hence, a niche market is a sub-sector of a market where specialist firms sell products to customers who demand a particular good or service.

ⓔ **3/3 marks awarded.** A single sentence is sufficient to gain full marks but if unsure with a definition it is best to define each term clearly.

**[22]** (125,000 + 120,000)/2 = 122,500.

ⓔ **3/4 marks awarded.** Although the answer is correct, a mark has been lost because the whole range of numbers from which the calculation has been made has not been shown: 18,000; 110,000; (120,000; 125,000); 140,000; 170,000. With six numbers, it is impossible to identify a single middle number, so we take the two middle numbers (120,000 and 125,000) and average them. The answer is thus 122,500.

**[23]** The first significant point of comparison is that UberX charges a cheaper fare per three mile ride than taxis or UberLUX in each of the six cities. In Boston, for example, UberX charges $11 for a three mile ride compared to $22 by taxis and $29 by UberLUX. The second significant point of comparison is that Los Angeles is the only city where taxis charge higher fares than UberLUX. Taxis charge $27 for a three mile ride whereas UberLUX charge $25. In the other cities UberLUX charge higher fares.

ⓔ **4/4 marks awarded.** This answer has a clear structure and makes two significant points of comparison, supported with evidence from the extract.

**[24]** By limiting the supply of Black Cab licences the supply of Black Cabs is inelastic, hence if there is an increase in demand prices will rise significantly.

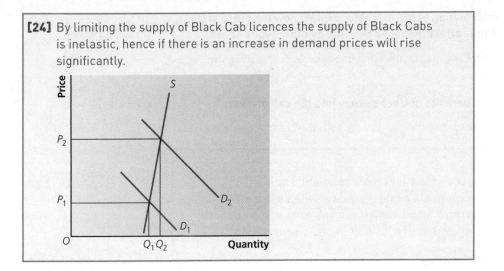

ⓔ **4/4 marks awarded.** A correctly drawn diagram with accurate labelling and equilibrium points identified.

**[25]** The main effect of Uber entering the cab market is to increase the level of competition and bring fare prices down. Traditionally Black Cabs in London have had limited supply and have been able to prevent competition from entering the market through a licensing system. This has acted as a barrier to market entry.

However, Uber has used smartphone technology to enable consumers to book drivers through their phones. This has increased the level of competition in the market because it is 'destroying the monopoly power of Black Cab drivers' (Extract B, lines 23–24). This should bring the price of fares charged by mini cabs and Black Cabs down because if they do not offer lower prices they will not attract customers who will otherwise use Uber.

This can be seen in the diagram below. As Uber enters the market the supply of cars offering passengers rides increases and the supply curve shifts to the right. Initially excess supply will appear as taxis seek to charge customers the higher fares at $P_1$. However, the market will be in disequilibrium and they will have to cut their prices to $P_2$ in order to sell their service to passengers.

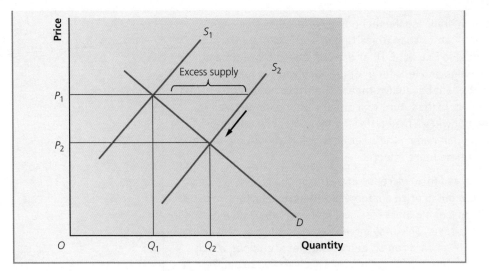

**ⓔ 10/10 marks awarded.** This answer is focused on the question, displays sound knowledge of economic terminology, employs a diagram to support the explanation and also uses evidence from the extract. The analysis is clear and the chain of reasoning is logical – top Level 3.

**[26]** Uber is a cab firm that has used technological innovation to challenge the market structure of the taxi industry. It has used smartphone technology to enable customers to book cabs with drivers using satellite navigation systems. Customers can use their phones to pay for the service and rate their satisfaction with the service.

The main benefit of Uber's entry into the market is lower cab fares. As can be seen in Extract A, in each of the five US cities UberX offers passengers lower fares than taxis. This is a significant benefit because it enables customers to buy cab services at lower prices and keep more of their disposable income for other purchases. According to Extract C, lines 14–16, UberX is 40% cheaper than its rival Addison Lee and 30–50% cheaper than a Black Cab.

Traditional taxi drivers may suffer from the lower fares because they will experience a fall in income. This will be a cost to the Black Cab drivers of London mentioned in Extract B because they have invested several years of their life gaining 'the knowledge' (lines 6–7) so that they can offer a professional service to their passengers. However, the need for drivers to have an expert knowledge of city streets is no longer important because of the development of satellite navigation systems. This means that drivers do not need to invest in learning streets and routes to pass a test and gain a licence because the technology enables them to drive a passenger to the desired destination.

Moreover, drivers who embrace the technology offered by Uber can actually earn higher incomes than Black Cab drivers despite offering lower fares. According to Extract B Uber drivers 'spend more time on the road picking up earnings and less time off the road waiting for customers'. This is a significant benefit because it means that Uber has made the taxi industry more efficient. In the future taxi drivers will no longer wait for hours in a taxi rank but will instead allow the technology to take them to where the customers demanding their services are. This will mean that drivers will use their time more effectively.

Lower taxi fares may lead to an increase in traffic on the road and pollution. As taxi fares fall in price customers will have an incentive to use taxis more often. People using other forms of transportation such as buses or trains may switch to taxis. This may increase the number of cars on the roads. The vast majority of cars run on petrol and diesel engines which emit harmful emissions into the environment. This will lead to poorer air quality in cities which will harm the health of the people living in these areas. This will increase market failure because the pollution dumped into the environment is a negative externality and the harm caused to the health of ordinary citizens will not be reflected in the price of taxi fares. Hence, Uber's entry into the taxi market may have a major negative environmental impact and harm the health of the citizens of major cities.

Ultimately Uber's entry into the taxi market will push down prices and enable passengers to access a better service at a lower price. Black Cab drivers with a licence will find that they will have to lower their fares to remain competitive but if they embrace change they will find that technological innovations will make their industry more efficient. These benefits will significantly improve the industry and offer passengers a better service but it will come at the cost of poorer air quality. Lower fares will encourage more cabs onto the roads and it will result in more pollution being dumped into the air.

**ⓔ 23/25 marks awarded.** This is a strong Level 5 answer. The introduction sets out the key technological issues and evaluation is used early in the answer as the student prioritises the main issues. The analysis is well focused and evidence is used from the extracts to support the points being made. The student makes judgements based on logical reasoning. A diagram could have been used to explain the issue of negative externalities. There is a strong final judgement in the conclusion.

**ⓔ Total score: 47/50 marks = Grade A**

Student B

**[21]** A niche is a small part of a whole.

**ⓔ** **1/3 marks awarded.** While the student has provided a succinct definition of a niche, she has made no mention of a market. Remember, you must address both words in the question.

> **[22]** The median number is 113,833 approx, obtained from (18,000 + 110,000 + 120,000 + 125,000 + 140,000 + 170,000) = 683,000 divided by 6.

**ⓔ** **0/4 marks awarded.** Unfortunately, the student has correctly calculated the mean number, but not the median number, so no marks have been awarded.

> **[23]** A first point of comparison is that the fares for UberLUX are higher than taxi and UberX fares in all the cities except Los Angeles. A second point of comparison is that UberX fares are cheaper than taxi and UberLUX fares in all the cities.

**ⓔ** **2/4 marks awarded.** The two significant points of comparison are fine, but no statistical back-up is provided, so this is a maximum of 2 marks (1 mark for each of the two points of comparison).

**[24]**

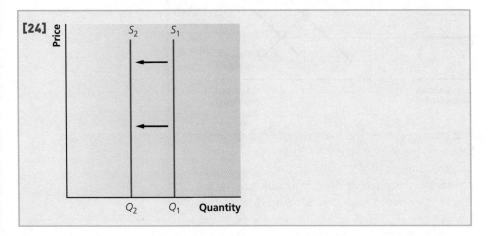

**ⓔ** **2/4 marks awarded.** While the diagram accurately depicts the likely change in supply conditions, by omitting a demand curve it does not show the likely effect on equilibrium price and quantity.

> **[25]** From a passenger's point of view, Uber cabs, Black Cabs and minicabs are substitutes for each other. If Uber attracts a lot of customers, because of its cheaper fares and/or the convenience of booking the Uber cab, the demand curves for Black Cabs and minicabs will shift to the left. Market forces will then bring their prices down.

**ⓔ** **5/10 marks awarded.** Overall, a Level 2 response. The answer earns half the available marks because the analysis is sound and relevant. However, to earn more marks, the answer needs more development, especially in terms of drawing on the information in the extracts, as the wording of the question indicates.

> **[26]** Economic theory tells us that the more firms there are in a market, the more consumers benefit because the market becomes closer to the economist's model of perfect competition. Perfect competition is defined by the following characteristics: a large number of buyers and sellers, each with perfect market information, but with each buyer and seller having to accept the ruling market price while being unable to influence this price by its own actions. Finally, there are no barriers to entry or exit in the long run. What happens in a perfectly competitive market, for both a firm within the market and the whole market, when new firms enter the market is shown in the following pair of diagrams:
>
> **(a)** One firm in the market    **(b)** The whole market
>
>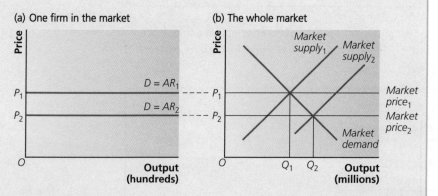
>
> Uber's entry into the cab market causes the market supply curve to shift rightward, from *Market supply$_1$* to *Market supply$_2$*. This brings down the price of cab fares so all consumers benefit. However, the falling price of fares means that cab drivers will probably suffer. They will experience lower income and will probably have to work longer hours to try to recover their previous earnings.

**ⓔ** **18/25 marks awarded.** As with the answer to the previous part of the question, the analysis is sound and relevant. However, the student should have made the point that, although the cab market would become more competitive, it would still fall short of perfect competition, if only because Black Cabs will still be regulated by a government agency. The answer also needs to discuss in more depth how consumers, cab drivers – and also perhaps the government – might enjoy benefits and suffer costs from Uber's entry into the cab market. A 'winding up' concluding paragraph is also needed. However, the answer reaches Level 4 in the mark scheme (16–20 marks) for displaying 'sound, focused analysis and some supported evaluation'.

**ⓔ** **Total score: 28/50 marks = Grade C**

# Question 4 What is a public good? (A-level)

## Context 1

Total for this Context: 40 marks

Study Extracts A, B and C and then answer all parts of Context 1 that follow.

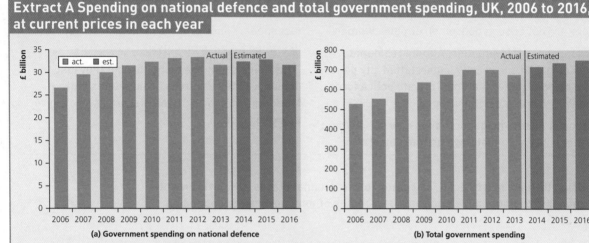

**Extract A Spending on national defence and total government spending, UK, 2006 to 2016, at current prices in each year**

(a) Government spending on national defence

(b) Total government spending

## Extract B Is a road a pure public good or a quasi-public good?

What is a public good? We know that markets generally provide private goods, but markets may not be able to provide public goods. Private goods of course include merit goods, but merit goods must not be confused with public goods. [5] Public goods are recognised as having benefits that cannot easily be confined to a single buyer (or set of buyers). Yet once public goods are provided, many people can enjoy them for free. For individuals pursuing their own self- [10] interest, it is often the best and most rational strategy to let others provide the good and then enjoy it free of charge. It is this which leads to market failure.

However, some goods such as roads are better [15] thought of as quasi-public goods rather than as pure public goods. With a quasi-public good, it is possible to use prices to exclude free-riders, though very often there is a case for not doing so. With roads, one compromise is to [20] charge motorists for driving their cars during rush hour, but to allow free use of the roads at uncongested times.

Source: adapted from news sources, 2015

### Extract C Paying for protection

About 11 pm, one dark evening, Mrs Muffie Michaelson of Atlanta, Georgia, went to the door of her garage to make sure it was secure. As she looked outside, she was shocked to see a man rifling through her car. She later said: 'We don't get any police patrolling in our neighbourhood. There are not enough policemen or policewomen.' [5]

In response to this situation, Atlanta residents, frustrated with chronically understaffed city police, are piecing together their own private police force, neighbourhood by neighbourhood. [10]

Dozens of Atlanta neighbourhoods now supplement Atlanta police with their own private patrols. In some cases, businesses are paying extra taxes to create a private agency they control. In others, [15] homeowners are selling memberships to their own neighbourhood police departments which employ off-duty Atlanta officers to tackle street-level crime like burglary, car break-ins and thefts from tool sheds. These officers can make arrests just [20] like when they are on duty.

'The police should be doing this but they just don't have the resources,' said Atlanta citizen Mark Romzick. 'The private security patrols give us extra comfort.' [25]

Source: adapted from news sources, 2015

---

**[01]** Using the data in Extract A, calculate, to two decimal places, UK government spending on national defence as a percentage of total government spending in 2013. [2 marks]

ⓔ This question asks for a simple percentage calculation. Remember to include the % sign in your answer and state your answer to two decimal places. 2013 was probably chosen as the date for this question as it was the last year of actual data in the graphs. The data for 2014, 2015 and 2016 are estimated data, which are generally not as accurate as actual data.

**[02]** Explain whether it can be concluded from the data in Extract A that real expenditure on national defence was expected to fall in 2016, compared with its total in 2015. [4 marks]

ⓔ This question is testing your understanding of the difference between nominal and real data and about what can be inferred or concluded from the data themselves, without the help of any extra information.

**[03]** Extract B (lines 3–5) states that merit goods are examples of private goods, but merit goods must not be confused with public goods. What is the difference between a public good and a merit good? With the help of an appropriate diagram, explain why market provision may lead to too little consumption of a merit good such as education. [9 marks]

ⓔ Make sure you answer both parts of the question. The first part carries relatively few marks because it is testing the lower-order skill of knowledge and understanding. Nevertheless, students often confuse merit goods and public goods. The second part carries more marks because it is testing the higher-order skill of analysis, and also because an appropriate diagram must be included in the answer.

**[04]** Evaluate the case for and against providing police services solely through government spending and outlawing the private provision of security services. [25 marks]

(e) Part [04] questions, which ask for evaluation of an issue or issues set out in the wording of the question, often include 'weasel words' such as *must*, *always*, *never* and *inevitably*. In this question the 'weasel word' is *solely*. When 'weasel words' are in the question, good answers always focus on them. As a general rule, it is best to write an answer that takes issue to a certain extent, but not completely, with the central assertion of the question.

---

**Student A**

**[01]** (£32bn/£675bn) × 100 = 4.74%.

In 2013 UK government spending on defence was 4.74% of total government spending.

---

(e) **2/2 marks awarded.** Full marks for the correct answer with the correct sign. It is always advisable to show your workings.

---

**[02]** It is not possible to conclude from the data available that real expenditure on national defence will fall in 2016. Real expenditure can be calculated only if inflation data are available and subtracted from nominal spending. Given that nominal spending on defence is estimated to fall from £33bn in 2015 to £32bn in 2016 it is likely that real expenditure will fall. However, if the average price level is negative and prices are falling at a faster rate then it is possible that real expenditure could be rising.

---

(e) **4/4 marks awarded.** This gives a clear answer to the question asked. It explains the information needed to calculate a fall in real expenditure on national defence and the reason why conclusions cannot be drawn.

---

**[03]** Public goods and merit goods are both examples of market failure and their production and consumption are desirable as they help create a better society. The market struggles to provide a public good because of its three characteristics. Public goods are non-excludable, non-diminishable and non-rejectable. A lighthouse is an example of a public good because once it has created a light beam it cannot stop ships from seeing the light; it does not matter how many ships see the light; and the lighthouse owner is unable to prevent ships from free-riding on the service.

Merit goods in contrast are excludable and diminishable. Schools and universities can exclude pupils from classes. Private schools often charge high fees on the justification that smaller classes lead to better teaching because the quality of a lesson is diminished by larger class numbers.

When left to the market merit goods are under-consumed because of information problems. Too often individuals place too much emphasis on the short-term costs of paying for a merit good and do not appreciate the long-term benefits. High levels of university tuition fees are often said to create disincentives to higher education study to students from

---

lower income households. As a result too few people do not invest in their education and gain the skills and qualifications that enable them to benefit from higher paid employment in the long run. This can be seen in the diagram below where if left to the free market only $Q_1$ will be consumed.

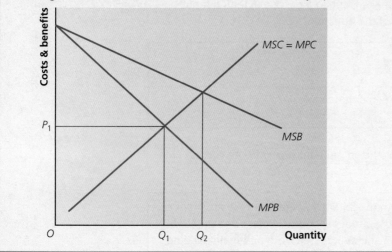

**Exam tip**

This diagram, which shows marginal private and social costs and benefits, is an A-level diagram. Candidates at AS are not expected to understand the diagram, which is explained in Student Guide 3.

ⓔ **6/9 marks awarded.** The distinction provided is accurate, but the explanation is somewhat confused. The written part of the answer explains under-consumption in terms of the divergence between short-run and long-run private costs and benefits, but this does not tally with the diagram, which shows private and social costs and benefits. The student has also written: 'As a result too few people do not invest in their education and gain the skills and qualifications that enable them to benefit from higher paid employment in the long run.' This is obviously wrong as he should have written: 'As a result too few people invest in their education and gain the skills and qualifications to enable them to benefit from higher paid employment in the long run.' However, treating this as a 'slip' rather than as a fundamental lack of understanding, only 1 mark is deducted for this mistake.

**[04]** The police force and private security services have characteristics of both private and public goods. The role of the police is, however, distinctly different from that of private security, so although it may be acceptable in a free society for households and firms to pay for private security services, only the government should provide the police force.

One of the main roles of a police or security service is the protection of private property. In this sense the service provided by the police has the characteristics of a private good. Households and firms pay for security officers to guard buildings and patrol land. Extract C gives examples of residents in the US city of Atlanta paying private police forces to perform this function. This is a simple market transaction where consumers pay for a clearly defined service.

Private security does have characteristics of a public good. Security patrols seek to prevent 'street-level crime like burglary, car break-ins and thefts from tool sheds' (Extract C, lines 15–20). The mere presence of a security patrol creates a deterrent to criminals. Whilst this provides benefits to the households and firms that have paid for the service it also benefits those who have not paid and are effectively free-riding. In this sense the police and security firms are quasi-public goods.

In a free society it is acceptable for security service to be provided by private sector firms. Companies such as G4S can sell security officers at commercial rates to guard property and patrol neighbourhoods. The legal powers that the State must retain for only government controlled and salaried police officers are the powers of arrest and prosecution.

If a market economy is to function efficiently it is essential that legal disputes, such as the ownership of property or the resolution of contracts disputes, are settled by a neutral legal system. This is because economic agents need to be confident that the market exchanges they enter into are free and voluntary. This requires a police force and legal system that obeys the rule of law and ensures that all criminal and legal matters are treated justly. If private security firms are allowed to arrest suspected criminals and pursue prosecutions they will be in danger of acting in the interests of the individuals and businesses that pay them. Hence governments should be the sole provider of the police force in society.

If the police force is not providing an adequate service for its households and businesses, like the situation in Atlanta, then citizens and companies should really use democratic means to change government policy. They should support tax increases aimed at improving the police force and not seek to employ over-powerful private security firms.

In conclusion, the police force and private security providers are quasi-public goods. It is acceptable for private firms to offer security services that guard buildings and patrol local areas. Only the police can be allowed to make arrests and pursue prosecutions under the instruction of government officials and in line with the law. This ensures the healthy functioning of a democratic capitalist society.

@ **23/25 marks awarded.** When a question includes the command word 'evaluate' students are required to make judgements based on the available evidence. The answer is well structured. The introduction attempts to apply economic theory to the context of the question and identifies the main characteristics of private and public goods. The answer analyses the issues and uses evidence from the extract to support the judgements made. It is always good to quote key words or phrases in the extracts and state which line they are from.

@ **Total score: 35/40 marks = Grade A\***

**[01]** (£32bn/£675bn) × 100 = 4.85.

ℯ **0/2 marks awarded.** The calculation is wrong, lying outside the range of tolerance for decimal places that might be allowed in the mark scheme. In addition, the % sign is missing. A mark is automatically dropped if units of measurement are not indicated.

**[02]** It is not possible to conclude from the data available that real expenditure on national defence will fall in 2016. This is because real data are data measured at current prices whereas nominal data are data measured at constant prices.

ℯ **1/4 marks awarded.** While the student's conclusion is the right one, his explanation is wrong and confuses real and nominal data. Because no correct evidence is quoted, only 1 mark has been awarded.

**[03]** Pure public goods are non-excludable and non-rival which markets cannot provide. Merit goods by contrast are private goods which markets can provide; however, they provide too little and merit goods end up being under-consumed. When an individual consumes a merit good, he or she discharges positive externalities which benefit other people, who are known as third parties. My diagram below shows how in a free market merit goods are under-consumed:

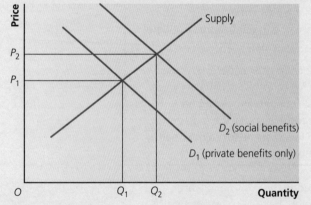

**Exam tip**

This is an AS diagram, but it is also acceptable at A-level.

My explanation is as follows: my diagram shows that in a free market, the price charged is $P_1$ and the quantity bought and sold is $Q_1$. However, the benefits to society exceed the private benefits enjoyed by consumers. The result is too little demand. $Q_2$, which is the socially optimal level of consumption, is greater than $Q_1$, the privately optimal level of consumption.

ℯ **9/9 marks awarded.** This is an excellent answer. Although the explanation could be developed more, it is accurate. The explanation includes the diagram that AQA expects students to be able to draw at AS level, though an A-level diagram such as the one included in the Grade A answer is equally permissible.

**[04]** In the UK, for well over a century, police services have been provided by local government on a regional basis. This is because policing is a necessary service. In London the Metropolitan Police (or the Met) is provided by the largest police authority in the UK. Government provision ensures for the most part a very high standard of service. Doubtless, there are 'rotten apples' in the constabulary and among higher ranked police officers, but on the whole, the 'bobby on the beat' is a friendly, honest individual who everybody trusts.

In economic jargon, the reason why the government provides police services is because policing is a public good. A public good is non-excludable and non-rival. For the police, this means that provided police services are provided, it is impossible to exclude people from gaining the benefits. If the service were to be provided by a market, people could 'free-ride', which means that they benefit from the service provided even though they may refuse to pay for the service. When this happens the incentive function of prices breaks down: there is no incentive to provide a service for which there is a need if everybody chooses to free-ride. Without a police force, crime would be even more rife than it is today. Hence the case for government provision.

However, as the question mentions, and as the extracts in the question show, it is possible to provide police services through the market. Again, in economic jargon, policing is a quasi-public good rather than a pure public good. As the Atlanta story in Extract C demonstrates, groups of private individuals can set up their own private police forces or security services to protect themselves from burglary. But there is a danger that the private provision of security services will lead to vigilante activity, with untrained or malicious security guards shooting innocent individuals in the back.

Evaluating the issues involved, I think that mainstream policing should only be provided by government. However, there is a strong case for allowing the market to provide 'fringe' policing activities, such as stewarding crowds at football matches and providing security guards at shopping malls and for the guarding of industrial premises on trading estates and business parks.

ⓔ **13/25 marks awarded.** The quality of this answer is extremely variable. The first paragraph, which is all about personal opinion, is devoid of any proper economic content. The second and third paragraphs are better. The student recognises that policing is a public good and defines the concept. He implies that if policing were to be regarded as a pure public good, there would be a case solely for government provision, but that as many policing services have quasi-public good properties, there is a case for their provision by private security firms. Although the analysis is rudimentary, the fact that there is a concluding paragraph takes the answer into Level 3 (11–15 marks): some reasonable analysis but generally unsupported evaluation. The concluding paragraph does not really add anything to the quality of the answer.

ⓔ **Total score: 23/40 marks = Grade C**

# Question 5 The market for cocaine: an example of a 'repugnant market' (AS)

## Context 2 Should there be legal markets in narcotic drugs?

Total for this Context: 50 marks

Study Extracts D, E and F and then answer all parts of Context 2 that follow.

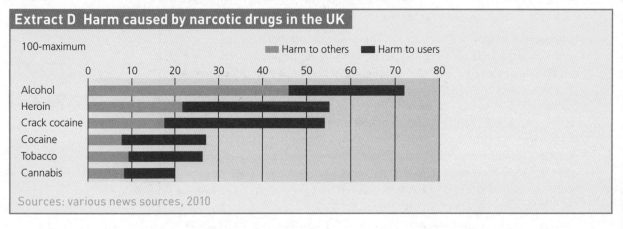

**Extract D  Harm caused by narcotic drugs in the UK**

100-maximum

Harm to others    Harm to users

Alcohol
Heroin
Crack cocaine
Cocaine
Tobacco
Cannabis

Sources: various news sources, 2010

**Extract E  Changes in the market for cocaine**

Increased competition in the cocaine trade has cut the profit made on the commodity to a very low level, considering the risks involved. The retail price of £40 per gram on London streets barely covers all the costs of producing powder cocaine in 5 Central and South America, wholesale costs and transport and distribution costs.

The falling price of powder cocaine is especially striking considering the supply problems of recent years. Global production of the coca leaf 10 is estimated to have fallen in every year between 1999 and 2004, from 353,000 tonnes to 236,000 tonnes. Unlike heroin, cocaine is perishable, which means it cannot be stockpiled against lean times.

The reason why the cocaine price has fallen so 15 much is that the market is opening up, with new criminal gangs entering the market. New supply routes have also been introduced, which makes it more difficult for the police to control entry into the UK market and drug trafficking within the UK. 20 The dissolving of mafia gangs, previously held together by ethnic and family bonds, is likely to mean still freer trade in illegal drug markets.

Competition in the drug market is good for the drug user, at least in the very short run, which means it is bad for anyone trying to reduce 25 or eliminate drug taking. Against Mafia-style cartels, the police might have succeeded. They are less likely to prevail against the invisible hand of the free market. 30

Source: news reports, 2015

## Extract F  Should the selling and consumption of narcotic drugs be made legal?

Fed up by the growth of deaths, crime and corruption generated by the world's illicit drug trade, a growing number of government officials and academic experts have begun to debate whether the consumption and sale of narcotic drugs such as heroin and cocaine should be made legal. Prohibition of these drugs may have failed. [5]

The legalisation argument rests on the assumption that drug laws, not drugs themselves, cause the most damage to society. If drugs were legal, the argument goes, drug black markets worth tens of billions of dollars would evaporate, the empires of drug gangsters would collapse, addicts would stop committing street crimes to support their habit, and the police, courts and [10] prisons would no longer be overwhelmed by a problem they cannot hope to defeat. [15]

But most politicians and policy makers disagree, cheaper, purer and far more widely available, and would cause a sharp jump in private costs to the drug users [20] and external costs imposed on society in general. They say the losses would far outweigh the gains.

A key question is how much does society pay because drugs are illegal and how much does society pay because drugs themselves are [25] harmful? Drug-related crime, such as child abuse and assaults by people experiencing drug-induced psychosis, will still exist, even if consumption is made legal.

Source: news reports, 2015

**[27]** Define the term 'private costs' (Extract F, line 20).  [3 marks]

ⓔ As in the earlier AS questions (Questions 1 and 3), make sure you define both words in the term, in this case 'private' and 'costs'.

**[28]** Using the data in Extract D, calculate, to two decimal places, the harm caused by cannabis consumption as a percentage of the harm caused by alcohol consumption, first for harm for the drug users, and second for harm to others.  [4 marks]

ⓔ Make sure you obey the instruction to calculate the answer to two decimal places. Note also that to gain all four of the available marks, you must make two calculations.

**[29]** Identify two significant features of the data shown in Extract D.  [4 marks]

ⓔ Significant features might centre on positions in the overall 'league table', differences between harm to users and harm to others, and comparison of harm caused by consumption of legally available drugs and drugs that are illegal to consume.

**[30]** Draw a supply and demand diagram to show the effect of changing supply and demand conditions on the world price of cocaine, according to the information in Extract E.  [4 marks]

ⓔ To answer this question, make sure you identify the parts of Extract E that are relevant to the question, while ignoring irrelevant material. Also, make sure you clearly label the axes on your diagram, the supply and demand curves and the coordinates showing price and quantity.

**[31]** Explain why many economists believe that narcotic drugs are demerit goods.  [10 marks]

ⓔ Make sure you define a demerit good in your answer, in terms of the negative externalities generated in consumption and/or in terms of the misinformation that occurs in the market for the good.

**[32]** Evaluate the case for and against legalising, but also taxing, consumption of
narcotic drugs

[25 marks]

ⓔ You must address both the issues posed by the question, namely legalising
consumption and taxing consumption of narcotic drugs such as cocaine.

---

**Student A**

**[27]** A private cost is the cost incurred by a firm when it produces a product,
excluding external cost, which may be passed onto society as a result of
economic activity. However, it might also be incurred by a consumer.

---

ⓔ **3/3 marks awarded.** The definition is correct and concise.

---

**[28] (i)** $(12/26) \times 100 = 46.15\%$
The harm caused by cannabis consumption as a percentage of the
harm caused by alcohol consumption on users is 46.15%.

**(ii)** $(8/46) \times 100 = 17.39\%$
The harm caused by cannabis consumption as a percentage of the
harm caused by alcohol consumption on others is 17.39%.

---

ⓔ **4/4 marks awarded.** Accurate calculations with full workings shown.

---

**[29]** The first significant feature is that alcohol causes more harm to others
than any other drug in the UK and cocaine causes the least harm to
others. According to the table, alcohol causes a harm score to others of 46
in contrast to cocaine's score of 7.

The second significant feature is that crack cocaine causes the most harm to
users, cannabis causes the least harm to users. According to the table, the harm
score to users of crack cocaine is 36 but the harm score to users of cannabis is 12.

---

ⓔ **4/4 marks awarded.** A clear structure and two significant features identified
and supported with evidence from the extract.

---

**[30]** New suppliers have entered the market and the increased competition has
pushed prices down.

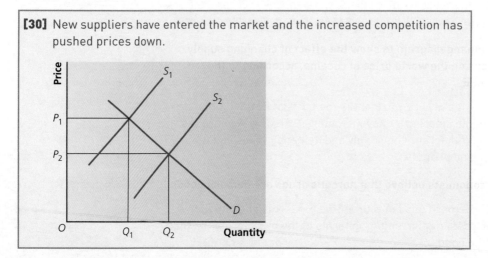

---

**ℰ 4/4 marks awarded.** A correctly drawn diagram with accurate labelling and equilibrium points identified.

> **[31]** A demerit good is defined as having rival, excludable and diminishable characteristics (i.e. they are private goods and not public goods) but when supplied by the free market will be over-consumed due to information problems. Narcotic drugs are an example of a demerit good because individuals choose to consume the good but give too much weight to the short-term benefits of consumption and not enough consideration to the long-term costs.
>
> Narcotics such as crack cocaine are highly addictive and although users will experience a short-term high they will suffer longer-term damage to their health through continued consumption. Crack cocaine is highly addictive and it is probable that the majority of users will develop an addiction.
>
> The long-term harm caused to society through narcotics is twofold. First, the consumption of narcotics will often result in higher levels of crime and violence as addicts will resort to theft to pay for their habits. According to Extract D the cost of negative externalities caused by crack cocaine on third parties has a score of 17. Second, harm inflicted by an individual on their own health as a consequence of crack cocaine consumption has a score 36. Individuals do not fully appreciate the long-term health risks of demerit good consumption because they cannot fully comprehend how the drug will affect their bodies over a long period of time.

**ℰ 8/10 marks awarded.** This is a well-organised answer. Key concepts are defined correctly and economic theory is applied to the context of the question. Evidence from the extract is used to support the analysis, but issues could have been developed a bit further and a diagram could have been included.

> **[32]** Narcotic drugs are demerit goods, the consumption of which results in negative consumption externalities being dumped on society. For many years harmful narcotics, with the exception of alcohol, have been banned in the UK. However, due to the increasing supply of narcotics in UK markets there is a case for legalisation of drugs so that the proceeds can be taxed, which can be used in turn to pay for treatments for users.
>
> The traditional argument put forward in favour of criminalising most narcotic drugs by the British government is based on principle. Narcotics such as heroin and cocaine are highly addictive demerit goods. When consumed by individuals narcotic drugs will create significant negative consumption externalities which result in harm to both users and third parties. This situation would be made worse by the legalisation of drugs because 'highly damaging substances would be cheaper, purer and far more widely available' (Extract F, lines 19–20).

Hence, for many years the policy of the British government has been to ban the possession and sale of narcotic drugs and punish offenders with significant prison sentences. This is a strong argument that is supported by many politicians, medical professionals, senior police officers and the majority of the public.

The case in favour of legalisation is based on practicality. The arguments put forward are twofold. First, the police can no longer enforce the ban and stop criminals from smuggling narcotics into the UK. According to Extract E, lines 17–20, new supply routes mean that it is more difficult for the police to control entry in the UK. The market has also become more competitive as small-scale criminal gangs have entered the market to compete with the traditional Mafia-style cartels. This provides greater problems for the police and makes enforcement less likely to succeed (Extract E, lines 27–30), thus legalisation should be considered because 'prohibition of these drugs may have failed' (Extract F, line 7). Morally this is a weak argument because it accepts that the government should allow individuals to consume drugs which will cause harm to third parties in society.

Second, legalisation will allow the government to regulate and tax the narcotics industry which is a more effective method of dealing with the harm caused by demerit goods. Extract F states that drug markets are worth 'tens of billions of dollars' (line 12) so if the government were to place taxes on narcotics similar to those on tobacco and alcohol the treasury could expect to raise billions of pounds in taxation revenue.

The taxation revenue can then be used to treat the problems caused by the negative externalities. Drug rehabilitation clinics will receive extra funding and the victims of drug-related crime could be paid compensation. Extract F claims that 'addicts would stop committing street crimes to support their habit' (lines 14–15) but there is no reason why this should happen. Legalising narcotics will not prevent addiction. Narcotics are still demerit goods and legalisation will not prevent significant harm being inflicted on users and third parties in society.

Ultimately the government has a choice. Morally narcotics are dangerous demerit goods that cause significant harm to society, therefore they should be banned and the police should use their powers to enforce the law. However, the practicality of drug laws has been diminished and governments may decide that if they cannot win the war on drugs they might be better to raise significant revenues from taxation and use the money to treat the harm caused by the addicts.

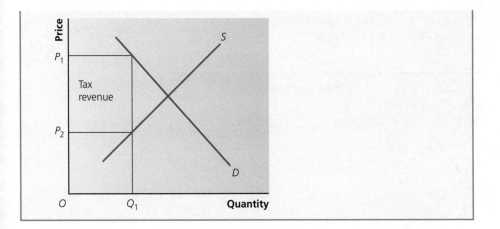

**ⓔ 23/25 marks awarded.** This is a good Level 5 answer. The key concepts are defined and explained in the introduction. The answer sets out key arguments and analyses issues using evidence in the extracts. The student could have used their own knowledge to develop arguments in greater depth. However, the answer addresses the question and provides a logical chain of reasoning.

**ⓔ Total score: 46/50 marks = Grade A**

### Student B

**[27]** A private cost is the cost incurred by a private individual.

**ⓔ 1/3 marks awarded.** An incomplete definition.

**[28] (i)** $(12/26) \times 100 = 46.95\%$
The harm caused by cannabis consumption as a percentage of the harm caused by alcohol consumption on users is 46.95%.

**(ii)** $(8/46) \times 100 = 17.39\%$
The harm caused by cannabis consumption as a percentage of the harm caused by alcohol consumption on others is 17.39%.

**ⓔ 3/4 marks awarded.** Percentage units of measurement are included, but the first calculation, to two decimal places, is inaccurate. Probably a slip by the student.

**[29]** Of the legal drugs, a possibly surprising feature is that alcohol is much more harmful, to both the user and to others, than tobacco. A second significant feature is that cannabis, though mildly illegal, is the least harmful of all the drugs shown in the table, both to users and to others. This surely means either that use of cannabis should be made legal, or that consumption of alcohol should be banned!

@ **2/4 marks awarded.** Two significant features are identified, but no figures from the data are used to provide evidence of each feature. The answer drifts into opinion.

**[30]**

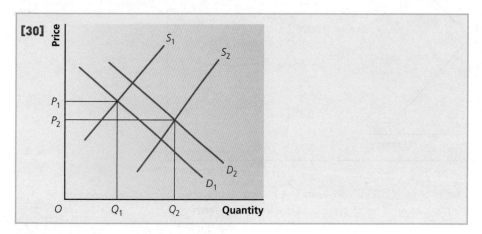

@ **3/4 marks awarded.** The student loses a mark because nothing is said in the extract about a rightward shift of the demand curve, though she has included it in the diagram. Nevertheless, because the demand curve has shifted by less than the supply curve, the diagram shows the price of cocaine falling.

**[31]** Demerit goods are basically goods that are bad for you. Economists are in favour of increasing economic welfare, utility or pleasure, but against decreasing economic welfare, disutility or displeasure. This is why economists believe narcotic drugs to be demerit goods.

@ **1/10 marks awarded.** This is a very weak answer. The student does not understand the meaning of the term 'demerit good' and makes a mistake common to many ill-prepared students when defining a demerit good as a good 'that is bad for you'. Instead, one of two definitions could have been given, in terms of social costs of consumption exceeding private costs of consumption, or in terms of imperfect information about the long-term private consequences of consuming a demerit good.

**[32]** Extract F states that a growing number of government officials are fed up by the growth of deaths, crime and corruption generated by the world's illicit drug trade .... and that 'the legalisation argument rests on the assumption that drug laws, not drugs themselves, cause the most damage to society. If drugs were legal, the argument goes, drug black markets worth tens of billions of dollars would evaporate, the empires of drug gangsters would collapse, addicts would stop committing street crimes to support their habit, and the police, courts and prisons would no longer be overwhelmed by a problem they cannot hope to defeat'.

That is the case for legalising consumption of narcotic drugs. The case against, as Extract F again states, is that 'highly damaging substances would be cheaper, purer and far more widely available, and would cause a sharp jump in private costs to the drug users and external costs imposed on society in general'.

In evaluating, my view is that the case for and against legalisation of drug consumption depends on which narcotic drug we are considering. As noted in an earlier answer, consumption of alcohol and tobacco is already legal, at least for adults. Many libertarians who believe in freedom of personal choice argue that the same should be true for cannabis.

There is much less agreement however on whether consumption of 'hard' drugs such as crack cocaine should be legalised. My personal view is against such legalisation.

If consumption were to be legalised, it would make sense to use other policy measures to deter or limit demand. Indirect taxation is the obvious policy to use – just as is the case with alcohol and tobacco taxation. However, for consumers, narcotic drugs are addictive products, which have highly price inelastic demand curves. This would mean that high indirect taxes might have little effect on the demand for narcotic drugs, but might be very good revenue raisers for governments.

In conclusion if the case for legalisation is accepted, the case for taxation is a more or less automatic follow up. However if the opposite case for maintaining the illegal nature of drug consumption is accepted, you can't legally tax an illegal activity!

ℯ **14/25 marks awarded.** Despite having displayed ignorance about the meaning of demerit goods in her previous answer, for this question the student has written a sound answer to which she has added a logical conclusion. However, while it is always a good idea to quote from the extracts, in this answer the student goes too far by copying out a much too long chunk of data. To rise above Level 3 (11–15 marks) the answer needs explicit application of demerit good analysis and at least one relevant diagram.

ℯ **Total score: 24/50 marks = Grade C**

# Question 6 Income and wealth inequality (A-level)

## Context 2

Total for this Context: 40 marks

Study Extracts D, E and F and then answer all parts of Context 2 that follow.

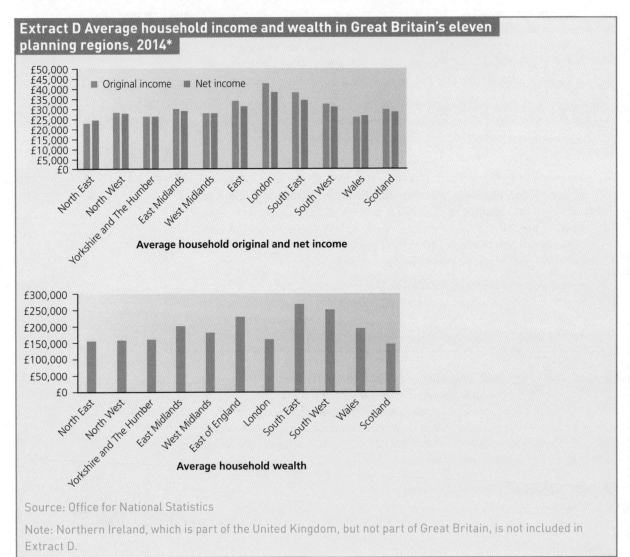

**Extract D Average household income and wealth in Great Britain's eleven planning regions, 2014***

**Average household original and net income**

**Average household wealth**

Source: Office for National Statistics

Note: Northern Ireland, which is part of the United Kingdom, but not part of Great Britain, is not included in Extract D.

## Extract E The scale of income and wealth inequality in the UK

The UK has a very high level of income inequality compared with other more developed countries. People in the bottom 10% of the population have on average a net income of £8,628. The top 10% have net incomes almost ten times that (£80,240). Income inequality is much starker at the top of the income scale, with the group with the ninth highest incomes making only 60% of the top 10%'s income. Inequality is much higher among original income than net income, with the poorest 10% having on average an original income of £3,875 while the top 10% have an original income over 27 times larger (£104,940).

Wealth in the UK is even more unequally divided than income. The richest 10% of households hold 44% of all wealth. The poorest 50%, by contrast, own just 9.5%. The bottom 10% of the population have less than £12,500 in total wealth, while the top 9% have £1,000,000 or more in wealth. Wealth is also unevenly spread across the different regions of the UK. An average household in the South East has almost twice (182.63%) the amount of wealth of an average household in Scotland.

Source: The Equality Trust, 2015

## Extract F

New OECD* research shows that when income inequality rises, economic growth falls. One reason is that poorer members of society are less able to invest in their education. Tackling inequality can make society fairer and the economy stronger. Rising inequality is estimated to have knocked nearly 9 percentage points off UK growth. Also, in recent years and particularly since the 2008 recession, young people have replaced the elderly as the group experiencing the greater risk of income poverty.

The most direct policy tool to reduce inequality is redistribution through progressive taxation and benefits. The OECD's recent analysis shows that redistribution *per se* does not lower economic growth. Of course, this does not mean that all redistribution measures are equally good for growth. Redistribution policies that are poorly targeted and do not focus on the most effective tools can lead to a waste of resources and generate inefficiencies.

Source: OECD reports, 2014

*The OECD is an international organisation which aims to promote policies that will improve the economic and social well-being of people around the world.

**[05]** List the 11 planning regions shown in Extract D in order of average original household income, from the lowest to the highest income, and calculate the average original household income in the median region. [2 marks]

**e** This question requires you to draw solely on the data of average household original income shown in the left-hand panel of Extract D. Ignore the data on net income and on wealth. There are two tasks to do here: first, to rank planning regions according to average household original income, and second, to identify the median average household original income. Make sure you don't confuse the median number with another measure of an average number, the mean.

**[06]** Using the data in Extract D as evidence, explain the difference between income and wealth, and also the difference between original income and net income. [4 marks]

**e** As only 4 marks are awarded for this question, work on the assumption that 2 marks are available for each of the explanations and that with each, 1 mark is for explaining the difference and 1 mark is for relevant use of the data.

**[07]** With the help of a Lorenz curve, explain how equality and inequality in the distribution of income can be shown on a diagram.

[9 marks]

ⓔ Make sure you answer both parts of the question. The first part carries relatively few marks because it is testing the lower-order skill of knowledge and understanding. The second part carries more marks because it is testing the higher-order skill of analysis, and also because an appropriate diagram must be included in the answer.

**[08]** Do you agree that progressive taxation and welfare benefits paid by the government to low-income households should be used to reduce inequalities in the distribution of income? Justify your answer.

[25 marks]

ⓔ Like all part [04] and part [08] A-level context questions, this question is testing your ability to evaluate. However, good evaluation should be preceded by good analysis, centring on the selection and application of one or more relevant economic theories.

---

**Student A**

**[05]** North East, Wales, Yorkshire and The Humber, West Midlands, North West, Scotland, East Midlands, South West, East, South East, and London. The median region is Scotland with an average original household income of £30,000.

---

ⓔ **2/2 marks awarded.** The student has correctly listed the 11 regions in the correct order and identified the median value. This is not a difficult question but requires students to understand data.

---

**[06]** Income is an economic money flow, which for households will normally take the form of wages and salaries, interest on savings and welfare benefit payments. Income is often paid either weekly or monthly and measured annually. Wealth is an economic stock of assets held by a household and accumulated over time. In Extract D the original average income of a London household is £43,000 whereas the average wealth is £160,000.

Original income refers to the income a household receives before taxation is deducted and welfare benefit payments are received. In Scotland the average household receives an original income of £30,000 but a net income of £29,000; in contrast in Wales the average household receives an original income of £26,000 and a net income of £27,000.

---

ⓔ **4/4 marks awarded.** The answer demonstrates good knowledge of economic concepts and uses the evidence in the extracts to provide examples.

**[07]** The Lorenz curve is an economic technique used in economics to measure inequality. The straight diagonal upward-sloping line which moves from 0 to 100 is the line of equality. This represents a society with an equal distribution of income.

However, the UK has a high level of income inequality. As Extract E states, the top 10% of earners in the UK have incomes 'almost ten times' higher than the people in the bottom 10% of the population. This is illustrated by the Lorenz curve which bends out. The UK will have a Lorenz curve that is further away from the line of equality than most other developed countries. This is because the UK has a higher level of income inequality than most other developed countries, such as Sweden.

The Lorenz curve:

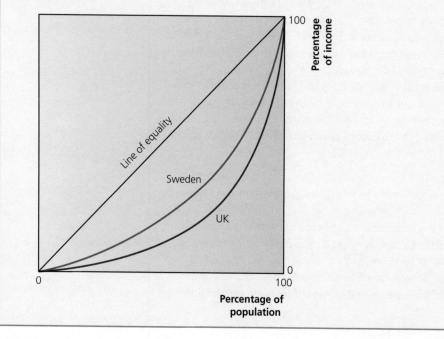

**ⓔ 6/9 marks awarded.** The diagram is clear and drawn correctly. The answer gives a reasonable explanation of the Lorenz curve and how it is used by economists. The answer addresses the question, evidence is used from the extract, but the issues could have been developed further. It is a high Level 2 answer because although the diagram is sound, the explanation of how the Lorenz curve illustrates equality and inequality could have been better.

**[08]** Modern advanced societies, such as the UK, have a taxation and benefits system that will to some extent transfer income and wealth from one section of society to another. Economists agree that some income and wealth should be taken from high-income and high-wealth groups and transferred to the poorest sections in society. However, there is a strong disagreement over the extent to which transfers should take place and the effect that it will have on the health of the economy.

Progressive taxation is when the government increases taxation rates as income increases. In the UK workers start paying income tax at 20% but this then increases to 40% and then 45% on earnings over £150,000 per year, although only 2% of the workforce pay the top rate of tax. In the tax year 2014–15 the British government collected £170bn from income tax. The UK welfare benefits system includes a number of payments such as Jobseeker's Allowance, Income Support, Child Benefit and Disability Benefit – many of them currently being replaced by Universal Benefit. The welfare budget is the largest of all government spending departments and in 2014–15 £232bn was spent on welfare payments.

Progressive taxation and welfare benefits will inevitably reduce the level of income inequality in the UK because the taxes paid by workers will be transferred to those claiming benefits, who are predominantly working in low-paid jobs or unemployed. However, the UK is still a deeply unequal society. According to the data in Extract E, lines 3–5, the poorest 10% live on an average income of £8,628 compared to the top 10% who have an average income of £80,240. Socialist economists argue that it is undesirable because the level of inequality is too high. They believe that income taxes on high-income groups should be increased in order to pay for higher welfare spending. In the 2015 General Election the Labour Party campaigned to raise the top rate of taxation to 50% to protect welfare spending.

Pro-free-market economists, however, argue that a more equal society is undesirable because it will damage economic growth and it is unfair. They accept that transfers of income are necessary to eliminate absolute poverty but believe that welfare benefits should only provide a minimum safety net. Neo-liberals do not believe that it is important to reduce the level of relative poverty by taxing high-income groups. According to neo-liberal theory the government should focus on incentives and encourage people to work by reducing the level of taxation and welfare benefit payments.

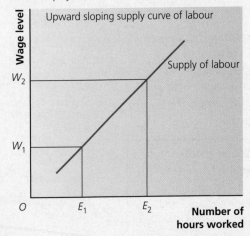

If the government cuts taxation this will effectively increase the wage level from $W_1$ to $W_2$ and the level of employment will increase from $E_1$ to $E_2$ in the diagram. This will incentivise workers to sell more labour and work longer hours. It will also make working relatively better paid than claiming welfare benefits. Hence low taxation not only rewards work but it also boosts employment. Chancellor George Osborne argues that the UK's recent strong economic performance stems from his policies that have increased the threshold at which low-income workers start paying tax, reducing the top rate of tax from 50% to 45%, and cutting welfare payments.

Nevertheless, if income inequality becomes too extreme it can hinder economic growth. Extract F says that research by the OECD shows that a high degree of income inequality means that 'poorer members of society are less able to invest in their education' (lines 3–4). This is a major problem for two main reasons. First, education provides the skills which enable workers to move into higher-paid employment. This allows individuals to lift themselves out of poverty and builds a stronger society. Second, if poorer sections of society are shut out of education the equity of society breaks down. Inequality is desirable if it creates incentives to work and rewards successful businesses but it is not justifiable if the poorer sections of society are locked into low-wage employment and poverty.

Therefore, government policy should not seek to redistribute income to create a more equal society but it should ensure that low-income households are not cut off from mainstream society and the opportunity to gain educational skills. Progressive taxation and welfare spending are necessary to eliminate the worst excesses of poverty but government should focus on strategies that ensure educational opportunities.

ⓔ **20/25 marks awarded.** This answer contains some good analysis and factual data. The student uses evidence in the extracts and his own knowledge. However, key terms are not defined fully and some of the points raised are not developed in sufficient depth in order to merit a Level 5 mark. The conclusion is reasonable but does not provide the examiner with a clear idea of which policies government could pursue to ensure educational opportunities.

ⓔ **Total score: 32/40 marks = Grade A/A\* boundary**

**Student B**

**[05]** London, South East, East, South West, East Midlands, Scotland, North West, West Midlands, Yorkshire and The Humber, Wales, and the North East. Scotland is the median region with an original household income of £30,000.

ⓔ 1/2 marks awarded. The student has listed the regions in the wrong order though he correctly states the median region and its average level of original income. Make sure you read all questions very carefully before you start your answers.

**[06]** The main difference between income and wealth is that income is a flow whereas wealth is a stock. Personal wealth is the stock, or historical accumulation, of everything you own that has value. By contrast, your personal income is the flow of money you receive hourly, weekly, monthly or annually, some of which (the part that you save) can add to your personal wealth.

The flowchart I have drawn below, which I have learned from an ONS article, shows the way net income (shown here as post-tax income) is derived from original income, shown in the top box. In the West Midlands, the two are the same, at around £27,000; in London original income is higher than net income by about £5,000, whereas in the North East, net income is higher than original income by about £2,000. In the poorer parts of the UK, cash benefits received by families exceed tax payments so net income is greater than original income. In richer parts of the UK, the reverse is true.

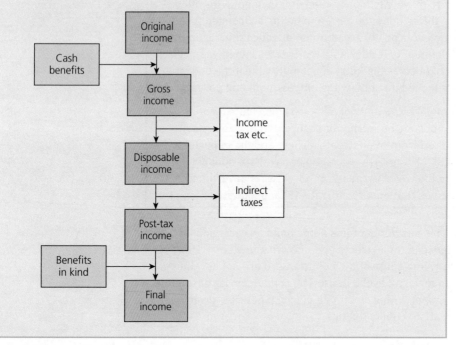

ⓔ **4/4 marks awarded.** This is an excellent if rather over-long answer, in which the student reproduces a rote-learned flow chart which would have taken a lot of valuable exam time to draw.

**[07]** The diagram below illustrates a Lorenz curve. The diagram shows complete income equality at tax rates of zero and 100%. Greatest inequality is shown at a tax rate of 50%.

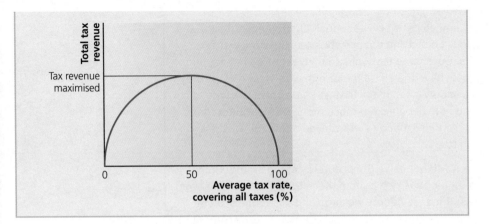

Tax revenue maximised — Total tax revenue — Average tax rate, covering all taxes (%) — 0, 50, 100

**e** **0/9 marks awarded.** This diagram displays complete confusion. The student has confused a Lorenz curve diagram, which is used to measure degrees of equality and inequality of income, with a Laffer curve diagram, which you may come across when studying the effects of different income tax rates on tax revenue. Students very often confuse the two curves; make sure you don't fall into this trap.

**[08]** If the government pursues a policy of higher taxation and higher welfare benefits it will effectively be transferring income from one group in society to another. This will have good and bad outcomes.

Socialist left-wing economists favour higher rates of tax and higher welfare benefits. The argument that they put forward is one of equality. For socialists equality is an important economic goal. They believe that equality is good and therefore government should do what it can to make people more equal, hence they believe that rich people should pay more tax and that this should be given to poor people in the form of welfare benefits. This policy has been pursued by the French president François Hollande who introduced a top rate of tax of 75% in France in order to raise money for the welfare benefits system.

However, I strongly disagree with left-wing economics and dislike all forms of government intervention in the economy. Higher taxes inevitably result in rich people leaving the country and living in tax havens such as Switzerland or Dubai. This is why lots of rich French business people now live in London. High taxation is bad because people who have worked really hard deserve to keep the money that they have worked for. High taxation is obnoxious and stops people from working. Welfare benefits should be kept low, otherwise everyone will stop working and will live off benefits.

In so far that there should be a welfare system, it should only be for those that deserve it. The state should provide a minimum safety net for the deserving poor, but not for the undeserving poor. Nevertheless, I am relaxed about poverty and do not worry too much about inequality. What government should do is encourage the private sector to train workers with appropriate skills. Government should also invest more in education to make sure that people have the skills that employers want so that they can get a job. This is a supply-side policy that will help solve the long-term problem of poverty and help people earn more money. This will let them get better paid jobs, earn more money and reduce inequality. This is a better policy than high taxes.

Higher taxes on the rich will not solve the problems of inequality. Higher taxes will lead to capital flight as rich people move to tax havens and avoid the taxes. This will result in less people working and economic growth stalling like it did in the 1970s under Labour governments. Government should therefore focus on supply-side policies that shift *LRAS* to the right.

ⓔ **15/25 marks awarded.** This answer is rather one-sided, sometimes on the verge of descending into a rant. However, it contains just enough economic analysis to enable a high Level 3 (11–15 marks) to be merited. Whatever a student's political stance, it is vital to consider opposing views in a neutral way, adopting the pose of a consultant advising a client.

ⓔ **Total score: 20/40 marks = Grade C**

## Knowledge check answers

**1** Scarcity means there is not enough of a good to meet demand. Economising means limiting the amount of a scarce good that you will buy and consume so as to be able to buy and consume other goods as well.

**2** At this moment, your opportunity cost is the 'next best' thing you could be doing instead of reading this guide.

**3** A shift of demand means the demand curve moves to a new position. An adjustment of demand means there is an adjustment along the demand curve in response to a change in price.

**4** Many people treat table salt as a necessity that must be used in cooking and for scattering on food. There are no close substitutes for table salt, so demand for table salt (as a generic product) is quite price inelastic. However, another brand of table salt, say the ASDA version, is an almost perfect substitute for Tesco's table salt. If Tesco increases the price of Tesco salt but ASDA leaves its price unchanged, some consumers may switch to the cheaper substitute. Demand for Tesco's salt is therefore more price elastic than demand for table salt as a generic product.

**5** The plus sign (+) tells us that the good is a normal good, i.e. demand for the good increases as income rises. The absolute size of the elasticity statistic (2.3) tells us that demand is income elastic. With this statistic, a 10% increase in income induces a 23% increase in demand. The good is also a *superior good* as well as a normal good. By contrast, an *inferior good* has a negative income elasticity of demand.

**6** The minus sign (−) tells us that good A and good B are complementary goods or goods in joint demand. A decrease in the price of good B causes consumers to buy more good B and also increases their demand for the complementary good, good A. The absolute size of the elasticity statistic (0.8) tells us the strength of the joint demand relationship. A 10% decrease in the price of good B leads to an 8% increase in the demand for good A. This is quite a strong joint demand relationship.

**7** Equilibrium is a state of rest or a state of balance between opposing forces. A market is in equilibrium when the amount consumers wish to buy exactly equals the amount producers wish to sell.

**8** Water is in composite demand since among its many uses are drinking, cooling, heating, cooking and washing.

**9** Production is what is produced, or output; productivity is output per unit of input.

**10** Output can grow at a faster rate than inputs into the production process.

**11** Workers perform simple repetitive tasks which would be better performed by machines such as robots. As a result the workers become deskilled and lose any pride in the job that they might otherwise have had.

**12** Total revenue is the income received by a firm when it sells its output; total profit is total revenue minus total costs of production.

**13** A market involves people or firms buying and selling goods or services in a voluntary way. Market structure may contain more than one firm and it refers to the number of firms in the market and their competitiveness.

**14** A large number of buyers and sellers, each with perfect market information, each able to buy or sell as much as they wish at the ruling market price, but unable by their individual action to influence the ruling market price, a uniform product, and no barriers to entry or exit in the long run.

**15** Profit maximisation is producing the level of output at which profit (revenue minus costs) is greatest; revenue maximisation is producing the level of output at which sales revenue is greatest.

**16** Strictly defined, monopoly exists when there is only one firm in a market or industry (pure monopoly). However, virtually all real-world firms can exercise a degree of monopoly power, though the ability to exercise monopoly power increases the fewer the number of firms in the market. An example of monopoly power is a firm using advertising and/or its brand image to persuade customers to buy its products and not to bother too much about the price they pay. In summary, monopoly is one firm only in a market; monopoly power is the power of a firm to act as a price maker rather than as a price taker.

**17** Resources can be misallocated in two main ways. They can be allocated in a productively inefficient way with the result that resources that could be better used elsewhere are tied up in a particular market or industry. They can be inefficiently allocated to consumers, resulting, for example, in under-consumption and hence under-production of merit goods and over-consumption and over-production of demerit goods.

**18** Tap water is supplied through a network of pipelines fed by reservoirs, both of which are owned by the water company serving the local region. Each water company serves a particular river system from which it gets the water it feeds into its reservoirs and pipeline network. For example, Thames Water supplies water to most people living in London. Having two or more water companies serving the same houses and businesses, each with its own storage and distribution system, would be unnecessary duplication, which would significantly raise costs. Hence, water companies are natural monopolies.

**19** Price competition occurs when firms compete against each other, for example to gain market share, by reducing prices below what other firms are charging. Quality competition occurs when firms compete against each other, by improving the quality of the goods or services they are selling, for example by improving reliability or improving design.

**20** Instead of paying for a broadband subscription, a student accesses his neighbour's browser, thereby enjoying free use of the internet.

**21** Television programmes are examples of quasi-public goods. BBC and ITV programmes are public goods in the sense that anyone can watch them, providing they have access to a television set. However, companies such as Sky broadcast their programmes as private goods, via satellite and cable. People who are unwilling to pay for the programmes cannot access them – unless they break the law or watch the programme in a public house.

**22** A merit good such as education or healthcare possesses two characteristics. In the first place, when people consume merit goods they generate positive externalities which benefit other people. In the second, consumption of a merit good is characterised by an information problem: consumers tend to ignore or underestimate the long-term private benefits of consumption. Likewise, public goods possess two characteristics: non-excludability and non-rivalry.

**23** Some pro-free-market economists agree with the libertarian view that people should be allowed to do whatever they want to do – providing they don't harm other people. They reject the concepts of merit goods and demerit goods, arguing that the two concepts legitimise unnecessary interference in people's freedom of choice. The state becomes a 'nanny state'.

**24** Equality is a positive term that can be measured. Equity is a normative term based on what is considered to be fair or just.

**25** In the case of a pure public good such as national defence, it is impossible to provide the good to one person without the rest of society also benefiting. This property of 'non-excludability' means that people can free-ride, benefiting from the good without paying. If too many people choose to free-ride, the incentive function of prices breaks down and it becomes impossible to operate a market. A missing market results.

**26** A price ceiling, or maximum legal price, has no effect on a market, providing it is set at a level above the equilibrium price in the market. However, if the price ceiling is imposed *below* the equilibrium price, then provided it is enforced and policed, it will distort the market. Excess demand is created which, in the absence of the price ceiling, would disappear as the price rises towards equilibrium. However, enforcement of the price ceiling prevents this happening. Queues or waiting lists result. These can then lead to the emergence of an illegal secondary market or black market.

**27** The most extreme form of regulation is to make it illegal to emit an externality such as pollution. Lesser forms of regulation are restrictions on time of day or year when it is legal to emit the externality, maximum emission limits, and forcing polluters to invest in clean technology.

**28** Prices provide information that allows all the traders in the market to plan and coordinate their economic activities. This is the signalling function of prices. The information signalled by changing relative prices creates incentives for people to alter their economic behaviour. This is the incentive function of prices.